THE BEST OF
JAZZ SCORE

Compiled By
Roy Pellett

BBC BOOKS

AUTHOR'S ACKNOWLEDGEMENTS

I would like to acknowledge the unfailing assistance of the various librarians who have worked on the Radio 2 desk in the BBC Gramophone Library over the years, and thank Elli for her co-operation and Karen for turning my scribble into a disc.

The author and the publisher would like to thank the following for their permission to reproduce copyright material:
George Melly, Humphrey Lyttelton, Ronnie Scott, Benny Green, Acker Bilk, George Chisholm, Chris Barber, Beryl Bryden, Peter Ind, Bob Wilber, John Dankworth, Dick Charlesworth, Monty Sunshine, George Webb, Kenny Baker, Diz Disley, Eddie Harvey, Alan Clare, Roger Horton, John Barnes, Campbell Burnap, Geoff Nichols, Digby Fairweather, Alan Elsdon, Jack Parnell, Yank Lawson, Dave Shepherd, Jack Fallon, Ian Christie, Max Jones.

The author and the publisher have tried to trace the remaining contributors or their estates (see below) without success. They apologise if they have infringed copyright and would be pleased to hear from them.

Eddie Thompson, Barney Kessel, Slim Gaillard, Herb Ellis, Buddy Rich, Peter Clayton, Al Cohn, Don Lanphere, Alex Welsh, James Moody, Mundell Lowe.

PHOTOGRAPH ACKNOWLEDGEMENTS

© BBC p. 1; Courtesy Humphrey Lyttelton/EMI Records p. 124; Max Jones/Dat's Jazz Picture Library pp. 20, 26, 67, 114, 116, 141, 155–158; © Radio Times p. 56; Redfern's/David Redfern pp. 17, 23, 37 (Suzi Gibbons), pp. 39, 53–55, 63, 75, 78, 81 (Bob Willoughby), pp. 85, 88 (Beryl Bryden), p. 94 (William Gottlieb), pp. 96–104, 123, 131 (Bob Willoughby), pp. 133–137, 144; Rex Features p. 40; Val Wilmer pp. 15, 61, 65, 70, 73, 150; Western Morning News p. 119

▶ *Title page* An Eton educated ex-Grenadier Guards officer meets a saxophone player who took lessons from Vera Lynn's father-in-law and his friend who edited the complete Wisden Anthology of Cricket. Of course, it is Humphrey Lyttelton, Ronnie Scott and Benny Green.

Published by BBC Books,
a division of BBC Enterprises Limited,
Woodlands, 80 Wood Lane, London W12 OTT
First published 1992
© Roy Pellett and Contributors 1992
ISBN 0 563 36326 6
Front Cover photographs © BBC
Set in 11/14pt Bembo Roman by Butler & Tanner, Frome
Printed and bound in Great Britain by Butler & Tanner, Frome
Jacket printed by Belmont Press, Northampton

CONTENTS

EDITOR'S NOTE

I retired from full-time touring in early 1980 after twenty years 'on the road', but soon found an element missing in my new life – humour.

With this in mind I wrote to BBC Radio expressing the opinion that there was a totally untapped source of humour in the country which I was positive would entertain their listeners. My letter landed on the desk of Richard Willcox, a senior producer in the Light Entertainment Department. Richard is a jazz trombonist and needed no convincing at all, so *Jazz Score* was born. A pilot show was recorded before an audience in October that year which ultimately became the opening programme of series 1, launched on 10 November 1981. At the time of writing a further thirteen series have been broadcast.

Richard Willcox has secured the services of various American musicians whenever it has been possible for them to fit a *Jazz Score* appearance into their busy touring schedules, and it has been an honour for me to work alongside the likes of Buddy Rich, Slim Gaillard and Barney Kessel. However, when you are faced with preparing a twelve-week series, you need a rock-solid foundation of regular guests whom you can rely on to be both entertaining and well informed week after week. We had three masters of the art: Humphrey Lyttelton, Ronnie Scott and our resident chairman, Benny Green.

More than fifty guests have appeared on the programme since 1981 and I have used material from most of them. These are, in alphabetical order:

KENNY BAKER Britain's number 1 trumpeter since playing in Ted Heath's orchestra in the immediate postwar years. Although he has spent much of his life as a studio musician, he has always found time to emerge regularly for a concert tour or jazz recording session to remind everybody of his world-class talent.

CHRIS BARBER Bandleader and trombonist. His astute business sense has kept his band at the top of the tree ever since his recording successes in the late 1950s helped spark off the Trad boom both here and in Germany. He challenged the orthodox Trad fans in the 1960s by using an electric rhythm section, which appealed to the emerging Blues audience.

JOHN BARNES Clarinet and saxophone player. He left Manchester and the Zenith 6 in 1955 to join Mike Daniels in London, where he has lived ever since. He is best known for his work with Alex Welsh in the 1960s and 1970s and Humphrey Lyttelton in the 1980s, and is rated world-class on baritone sax.

ACKER BILK Bandleader, clarinettist and vocalist. He started with the Ken Colyer band in the mid-1950s but soon formed his own band, whose cult following was in the vanguard of the Trad boom (1959–63). His humour is as broad as his clarinet tone, which has graced dozens of recordings with strings, notably on his composition 'Stranger on the Shore'.

BERYL BRYDEN Vocalist and washboard player. Britain's 'Queen of the Blues' is one of the best-known figures in European jazz. She turned professional when she went to Paris in 1953 and has been touring the world ever since. Her chromium-plated washboard helped Lonnie Donegan have a world-wide hit with 'Rock Island Line'.

CAMPBELL BURNAP Trombonist, vocalist and broadcaster. He played in Australia and New Zealand before coming home via New Orleans in the 1960s. He has subsequently played with Terry Lightfoot, Monty Sunshine, Alan Elsdon and Acker Bilk. His solo act is enhanced by his relaxed singing.

DICK CHARLESWORTH   Tenor saxophonist and clarinettist. He led his own City Gents at one time, and later worked
on P & O liners. In the 1970s he ran a bar in Spain which
proved very popular with holidaying musicians, but is once
again a regular face on the London jazz scene.

GEORGE CHISHOLM   Trombonist and arranger. Who
can dispute Leonard Feather's description of George as 'a super-
lative musician with an ageless style'. He was immensely popular at one time with his musical clowning.

IAN CHRISTIE   Clarinettist and journalist. He co-led the
Christie Brothers Stompers with his brother Keith and also
played with the Humphrey Lyttelton and Mick Mulligan
bands. He is a respected film and TV critic who still plays
around London.

ALAN CLARE   Pianist. Normally a soloist, he has worked
regularly with Stephane Grappelli. He has also performed with
Benny Carter, the Mills Brothers and Spike Milligan.

PETER CLAYTON   Broadcaster, journalist, writer and
critic. He was one of the best-known voices in jazz broadcasting
as well as being a very well-informed critic.

AL COHN   Tenor saxophonist and arranger. In the late 1940s
he worked with Buddy Rich, Woody Herman and Artie Shaw.
He was best known for his partnership with Zoot Sims.

JOHN DANKWORTH   Bandleader, alto saxophonist,
composer and arranger. He is best remembered for his Seven
(1950–3) and his big band (1953–64) which featured singer
Cleo Laine, whom he married in 1958. After this, apart from
acting as musical director for Cleo Laine on her world tours,
he increasingly worked in the studio, writing film music.

DIZ DISLEY   Guitarist, banjoist, cartoonist and raconteur,
a character of the postwar British jazz scene. He has played
with many bands but he is most at home with 'Hot Club'
string quintets. After he reintroduced Stephane Grappelli to
British jazz fans his groups backed the violinist for many years.

HERB ELLIS   Guitarist. He started with big bands such as Jimmy Dorsey's, played with Oscar Peterson (1953–8), then backed various singers including Ella Fitzgerald. After that he spent more time in the studio but recently he has been a member of the Great Guitars with Barney Kessel and Charlie Byrd.

ALAN ELSDON   Bandleader and trumpeter. He worked with Cy Laurie and Terry Lightfoot in the 1950s and formed his own band in 1961 which he has run ever since. In 1978 he began his long association with Keith Nichols when he joined the Midnite Follies Orchestra.

DIGBY FAIRWEATHER   Cornettist, broadcaster, writer and educator. The best-known jazz cornet player in Britain, he is equally at home playing 1920s jazz as he is alongside Don Rendell and Roy Williams. He is fast becoming a Radio 2 'Jazz Voice', and he is co-director of the educational organisation Jazz College with Stan Barker.

JACK FALLON   Bass player, violinist and agent. He arrived in Britain with the Canadian Air Force in 1944 and soon after joined Ted Heath for two years. He has recorded with the cream of British talent over the years as well as working with top Americans on tour here such as Duke Ellington and Sarah Vaughan. Since 1952 he has run a successful agency and he also plays 'Country' fiddle.

SLIM GAILLARD   Vocalist, guitarist and pianist. His death in early 1991 brought an end to a most bizarre fifty-five-year career which included tap dancing in variety, his double act of Slim and Slam (Slam Stewart) featuring his jive-talk vocals, such hit songs as 'Flat Foot Floogie', starring in films like *Hellzapoppin'* (1942), working as a comedian and running an orange farm. He became a familiar face again after starring in the TV blockbuster *Roots* and in recent years he became a cult figure on the European jazz circuit.

BENNY GREEN   Broadcaster, writer, journalist, critic and baritone saxophonist. His background of playing with Ronnie

Scott, Jack Parnell and Tony Crombie plus his writing and broadcasting experience has made him the perfect chairman throughout the first thirteen series of *Jazz Score*. He is an MCC member and is devoted to cricket.

EDDIE HARVEY   Trombonist, pianist, arranger and educator. One of the most talented musicians to emerge on the British jazz scene since his debut with George Webb in 1943. He has played with 'everybody' including Freddy Randall, John Dankworth, Humphrey Lyttelton, Woody Herman and Maynard Ferguson.

ROGER HORTON   Club owner. Roger has run the 100 Club in Oxford Street since the mid-1960s, so he has played host to hundreds of artistes, from B. B. King to Bob Brookmeyer and from Acker Bilk to the Bebop Preservation Society.

PETER IND   Bass player and club owner. He moved to New York in 1951 and worked with Lennie Tristano, Lee Konitz, Coleman Hawkins and Buddy Rich, amongst others. After returning to London in the 1970s he started his own record label and studio. He runs his own club, the Bass Clef.

MAX JONES   Author, journalist and critic. A tall, pale figure with horn-rimmed glasses and perennial beret at any concert since the end of the war would prove to be Max Jones. His articles and reviews were at the heart of the *Melody Maker* before it became a pop tabloid.

BARNEY KESSEL   Guitarist and raconteur. Early in his career he worked with Charlie Barnet, Artie Shaw and Oscar Peterson. From the 1950s on he has combined studio work with making jazz albums and tours. Whenever he is in Britain we hope he is available for *Jazz Score* because of his wonderfully laconic sense of humour.

DON LANPHERE   Tenor and soprano saxophonist. At the age of nineteen he was playing with Fats Navarro. Later he worked with Woody Herman, Artie Shaw and Claude Thornhill, but from an early age he was dogged by the effects and consequences of heroin addiction. Since the early 1980s he has been totally clean.

YANK LAWSON   Trumpeter. He has been one of the great trumpet players throughout his career, which stretches back almost sixty years. Although he worked for Ben Pollack, Tommy Dorsey and Benny Goodman, he is best known for his polished Dixieland playing with Bob Crosby and the World's Greatest Jazz Band.

MUNDELL LOWE   Guitarist and composer. He started with Ray McKinley in 1945 and then worked with Charlie Parker, Billie Holiday, Red Norvo and Benny Goodman. He is a prolific writer of TV and film music, and is nowadays musical director of the Monterey Jazz Festival.

HUMPHREY LYTTELTON   Bandleader, trumpeter, clarinettist, composer, cartoonist, author, journalist and broadcaster. Humph has led a band since 1948 and has been the epitome of the best in British jazz by sticking to a policy so succinctly summed up in the title of his first book – *I play as I please.*

GEORGE MELLY   Singer, author and art critic. His book *Owning Up*, which described his days with the notorious Mick Mulligan band in the 1950s, is probably still the funniest book ever written by a jazzman. His stage charisma carries the gospel of jazz to audiences who would not usually listen to the music.

JAMES MOODY   Tenor saxophonist and flautist. He is best known for his various associations with Dizzy Gillespie, with whom he first played in 1946. He also plays alto sax, and achieved his greatest recording success ('I'm in the Mood for Love') on that instrument. Since the 1980s he has been in great demand for tours of Europe.

GEOFF NICHOLS   Trumpeter, vibraphonist and record shop owner. Geoff is a founder member of the Avon Cities Band, one of the oldest and best semi-professional jazz bands in the country.

JACK PARNELL Bandleader, drummer, vocalist and musical director. As drummer with the Ted Heath Orchestra for seven years after the war, he was at the heart of their show. He is often underrated as a jazz drummer because he spent twenty years leading house orchestras for television shows.

BUDDY RICH Bandleader, drummer and vocalist. He is most people's idea of the greatest jazz drummer who ever lived. He first went on stage with his parents' vaudeville act at the age of eighteen months and was dancing and drumming on Broadway when he was four. Despite suffering from heart problems from 1959, he continued playing with all the greatest stars for almost another thirty years.

RONNIE SCOTT Bandleader, tenor saxophonist, club owner and raconteur. Ronnie Scott was nineteen years old when he played with Ted Heath in 1946 but, like many of his contemporaries, he elected to work on the transatlantic liners during the late 1940s so he could hear the 'Bebop revolution' in New York. Since 1959 he has run Ronnie Scott's Club in Soho with his partner Pete King and has been responsible for bringing the world's greatest jazz musicians to London.

DAVE SHEPHERD Bandleader and clarinettist. Although he started by playing in the Dixieland bands of Freddy Randall and Joe Daniels, he is best known for his own Benny Goodman-style quintets. He also plays with the Pizza Express All-Stars.

MONTY SUNSHINE Bandleader, clarinettist and cartoonist. A founder member of the legendary Crane River Jazz Band in 1949, during the 1950s he was with Chris Barber, and the recordings of his clarinet features made them both household names. He has led his own band since 1960.

EDDIE THOMPSON Pianist. He attended the same school for the blind as George Shearing. One of the most gifted British piano players of the postwar years, he was capable of handling a wide range of styles. He worked in the USA from 1972 to 1982.

GEORGE WEBB Bandleader, pianist and agent. His wartime band, resident in the Red Barn, Barnehurst (South London), was the nursery for the postwar jazz revival and included musicians such as Wally Fawkes, Ed Harvey and later Humphrey Lyttelton. In the 1950s and 1960s he was active as an agent, bringing over such American blues artistes as Speckled Red and Jesse Fuller. In the 1970s he formed a new band.

ALEX WELSH Bandleader, cornettist and vocalist. From the mid-1950s until he died in 1982, Alex Welsh led a hard-swinging Condon-style group which became the automatic choice for backing American stars such as Earl Hines and Ruby Braff. Bud Freeman went as far as to say it was 'the best small band of its kind in the world'.

BOB WILBER Bandleader, clarinettist and soprano sax-ophonist. A native of New York, in recent years he has settled in the Cotswold Hills, from where he conducts his international affairs. He studied with both Sidney Bechet and Lennie Tristano, which demonstrates the wide range of his skills. In 1984 he re-created the early music of Duke Ellington for the movie *The Cotton Club* and he has recently done a similar job for a film on Bix Beiderbecke.

Roy Pellett

THE BRITISH JAZZ SCENE

PRE-1960

C hapter One deals with stories about British musicians and their life-style from the 1930s, when American artistes such as Fats Waller, Benny Carter and Coleman Hawkins recorded over here, to the postwar years. At that point, a new generation of jazz musician appeared, including Humphrey Lyttelton and Ronnie Scott, who pioneered the revival in jazz interest despite the fact that a Musicians' Union ban meant that American jazz bands were not allowed to perform in Britain from 1933 to 1957.

The ban was sparked off by Duke Ellington's Orchestra having a phenomenally successful week at the London Palladium in June 1933 and the subsequent announcement that a return visit had been negotiated for the following year.

The British MU immediately and successfully lobbied the then Ministry of Labour to refuse work permits to visiting bands as they realised there was a ready market in Britain for American bands whereas there was absolutely no interest in British orchestras in the USA.

One of the by-products of this ban was that passengers on transatlantic liners in the years just after the Second World War were entertained by a constant stream of young, British, modern jazz musicians who worked the boats in order to get to 52nd Street in New York to hear Charlie Parker and Dizzy Gillespie *et al.*

I remember Archie Semple very well because he used to play clarinet with us in the Mick Mulligan Band for a while. He had a wonderfully wry sense of humour. One day we were in the Scottish Highlands driving around, desperately looking for some obscure place where we had been booked to play. I seem to remember that the Mulligan Band were somewhat uninhibited in those days, and as we drove along this narrow lane somebody broke wind.

Anyway, a few minutes later it was decided that we were lost and that we should turn around and go back down this lane. At which point Archie was heard to remark, 'Oh God, do we have to drive through that again?'

George Melly

It's not generally known that I once, long ago, appeared in the radio series *The Archers*. It was a bit of a let-down because I was expecting a day out at Ambridge, instead of which they recorded me in my back garden in Swiss Cottage – a small garden overlooked by houses.

The BBC sound engineers set up a microphone in the middle of the lawn, and from there I was supposed to be the 'star' opening the Ambridge village fête. We did several takes because the producer kept telling me to shout louder. So there I stood in front of this solitary microphone in the middle of my lawn bellowing 'Ladies and Gentlemen . . .' at an imaginary crowd, while windows opened and heads appeared from every neighbouring house to see what this loony was doing.

Humphrey Lyttelton

You know that Bob Wallis had a glass eye. The way he played his trumpet, I was always amazed it didn't pop out. Mind you, that eye used to get everywhere. He would quietly slip it onto somebody's poached egg sometimes, or he would roll it into your salad when you weren't looking.

I remember one night after we'd finished a gig in Blackpool, everybody bought a bag of winkles to eat on the journey home. Naturally, Bob's eye got mixed up with the winkles and we

▶ 'Please don't talk about me one eye's gone'
Bridlington's most famous jazz sons: Bob Wallis (*trumpet*) and 'Avo'
Avison (*trombone*) playing a riverboat shuffle in 1960. Banjoist Hugh
Rainey was obviously prepared for low bridges in that hat.

spent most of the trip home on our hands and knees in the
dark, groping around a bandwagon full of winkle shells trying
to find his damned eye.

Acker Bilk

The alto sax player Derek Humble is unfortunately no longer
with us. I worked with him originally in the Jack Parnell Band,
and then off and on right through to the Kenny Clarke–Francy
Boland Big Band. During the 1950s he acquired the nickname
Raffles because, for a fee, he used to pick the lock on the gas
meters of the bedrooms of some of those dingy guest-houses
we used to stay in. His fee was half the contents of the meter,
which could be useful because it was often more than we were
earning.

Ronnie Scott

The first band I ever sat in with was Carlo Krahmer's. At that time they were resident at the Nut House Club in Regent Street, where there used to be a fight every Saturday night with incidental music.

Humphrey Lyttelton

Did you know that the banjo player with the Yorkshire Jazzband before Diz Disley was Peter O'Toole the actor?

Chris Barber

Kenny Graham and I were looking for a sleeping compartment on a train back from Manchester after a gig. However, the guard refused to give us one as he said my guide-dog might bite someone.

Kenny got hold of the guard by the lapels and said, 'Look, mate, if you don't find us a sleeper I can bloody well guarantee that I'll bite someone.'

Eddie Thompson

Did you know that Beryl Bryden played washboard on Lonnie Donegan's big hit of 'Rock Island Line'?

Beryl is very keen on eating, in fact she is the only person I know who takes a mouthful of soup before the waiter has put it on the table.

George Melly

Dickie Devere was a very fine drummer and Norman Burns, another drummer, was certainly his most ardent fan.

One night Dickie was playing at 100 Oxford Street with Kenny Graham's Afro Cubists, and, being rather tired and emotional, he took a four-bar break which only lasted three and a half bars. As usual, Norman Burns was standing by the stage with another drummer who had been dragged along to hear this genius. When this second guy turned to Norman Burns to point out that his marvellous Dickie Devere had only played three and a half bars, Norman retorted, 'The trouble is that Dickie's mind works quicker than yours.'

Benny Green

► 'There you are cock, all the volume and vulgarity of Freddy Randall with none of the technique.' Mick Mulligan and George Melly demonstrating their public school charm in the 1950s.

When I first joined the Mick Mulligan Band we had two banjo players. The first one was Bill Cotton, who liked a drink or four. I remember we had a party to celebrate that the next day we were setting off on our first tour of Scotland. Unfortunately, Bill Cotton finished off everybody's drinks after they had collapsed and consequently arrived one and a half hours late for the pick-up next morning. He apologised to Mick for being late, saying that he'd lost his voice. Mick informed him that he'd also lost his job, so we only had the other banjo player after that.

He was Johnny Lavender, who was a sweet young man with a terror of chickens, which made things rather difficult in Ireland where most dance halls seemed to have them in residence at that time.

George Melly

I played with George Webb during the latter War years but in 1946 I was called up to do my National Service in the RAF.

Just before I got out I received a letter from Freddy Randall offering me a job in his band when I got demobbed. I was actually trained as an engineer but I thought I may as well play with Freddy while I was on demob. leave before going back to the factory – I have to thank Freddy Randall that I am still on demob. leave over 40 years later.

I eventually left the band because I got fed up playing in F, B flat and E flat all night long so I went along to 'Club 11' and got into bebop with Johnny Dankworth.

Eddie Harvey

Lennie Hastings used to tell the story of when he toured Ireland with the Mick Mulligan Magnolia Jazzband, and the sole publicity on one job consisted of a small blackboard on which was chalked the legend 'Tonight – Muck Milligan and his Mongolian Jazz Boys'.

Digby Fairweather

The first film I was in was called *George in Civvy Street* (1945), which starred George Formby. I was with Johnny Claes's band and we all played soldiers who had just returned from the war. In the story, George Formby opens a pub and we are the resident band. I remember it well because I got £12 a week.

Ronnie Scott

I toured for many years with the guitarist Bill Bramwell, a very dear man. However, he did have many peculiarities and phobias – in fact he got into such a state at one time he went to an analyst who got him into knitting.

It was quite a sight in the bandwagon: this rather nervous man knitting away muttering about one purl, one plain, while the rest of the band were sprawled around him belching alcohol fumes all over the place and holding forth on what they might have done with the promoter's wife given half a chance – assuming the lady in question's cooperation, a most unlikely assumption.

George Melly

Did you hear about the time Dave Clifford was booked by this terribly posh 'hooray' lady from Knightsbridge to play for one of her select gatherings? He got there nice and early, set up his drums and had a smoke. Next thing, this upper-class hostess comes up to him and enquires if he is ready to start. 'Start?' he said. 'Where's the band?' 'I've booked you to accompany the gramophone,' she replied. 'Goodness gracious, I'm paying you enough.'

He didn't want to lose the money and the booze was flowing like water, so he accompanied some of the best bands on record during the course of the evening. As things drew to a close she asked Dave to play 'The Queen'. 'Sure,' he said, 'have you got the record?' 'Of course not,' she retorted. 'Play a roll on your drum thing and lead my guests in singing.'

Well, Dave had been bashing the drink all evening and was feeling a bit unsteady, but he started off this rather uneven roll and broke into an extremely slurred vocal on 'The Queen'. As it was going along he noticed how earnest everybody looked, and he started thinking about the ridiculous situation he had been in all night. This set him off laughing and he collapsed across his drums, helpless with the giggles. The society hostess was furious and told him to pack his traps and leave her house as quickly as possible.

Alan Clare

I played for Freddy Randall for 10 days in 1949. I remember going to bed in the early hours of December 31st and when I woke up it was well into January 1st. I missed the big New Year's Eve job so that was the end of that.

Benny Green

I broke into my honeymoon to play a recording session with Fats Waller in 1938. I know we recorded 'Flat Foot Floogie' amongst other titles. We were all London-based musicians. The drummer, somewhat surprisingly, was Edmundo Ros.

George Chisholm

In the early days of the Humphrey Lyttelton Band I remember an occasion when we were in Sheffield. It must have been just before Guy Fawkes' night because Micky Ashman, our bass player, had bought some fireworks, and as we were all walking along he lit one and threw it under Humph's feet. Humph jumped into the road and nearly got run over by a bus. You should have heard the Etonian language!

George Webb

▶ George Webb, father of the revivalist jazz movement in the early 40s pictured at the piano with his 'Dixielanders' at Decca Recording Studios in May 1945. *L to R*: Buddy Vallis, Derek Bailey, Owen Bryce, Wally Fawkes, Reg Rigden, Eddie Harvey and Art Streatfield.

When Graeme Bell and his band were over here in 1951 they got a booking in a hall called Barrowland in Glasgow. It was one of those places where, when the curtain goes up, you find a line of bouncers, arms linked, facing the audience. Well, everybody in London was telling them to be careful up there in Glasgow.

It is no secret that Australians are quite fond of a bit of aggro, so they set off in their coach and fists were clenched before they reached Watford. As it turned out, the first half was very quiet, just the odd crash of breaking glass, but basically they were ignored as nobody was interested.

During the second half, however, Graeme was playing away at the piano when out of the corner of his eye he saw a figure climb on to the stage and advance towards him. On the principle of 'Don't shoot until you see the whites of their eyes', he went on playing until the figure was right at his shoulder – then in one movement he turned round and let fly. An autograph book went one way, a pen the other. He'd laid out the only fan they had in the place.

Humphrey Lyttelton

I used to take trumpet lessons from Tommy McQuater, and one day I asked him what I should do to control my nerves before a broadcast. He told me that he'd got over the problem with the aid of 'Dr Bells'.

Alan Elsdon

I know this club very well. It has now been called the 100 Club for well over twenty years, but I remember when it was Feldman's, which was Victor's father.

During the war I met most of the Glenn Miller Band here – musicians like Mel Powell, Peanuts Hucko and, of course, Glenn himself. I'll never forget Mel Powell tinkering around with a tune at the piano. I said to him, 'That sounds interesting, you must teach me that.' It wasn't long before everybody knew it. It was 'How High the Moon'.

Kenny Baker

I lived a couple of streets away from the Feldmans. When I was about fifteen years old I used to go to jam sessions in their front room with Victor's brothers, who both played a bit. At that time Victor was about seven or eight years old.

Ronnie Scott

Many years ago I was playing a residency in Dundee with the Bertie King Band. It was very cold and I used virtually to live in a great big old overcoat. At the end of the job Bertie broke the band up as he was going back to Jamaica, but he did say he'd like to take me with him. As I wasn't a particularly good baritone player I asked him why. He told me Jamaica was so hot I could throw away my dreadful overcoat.

Benny Green

Diz Disley is a remarkable person; he's made me laugh a great deal over the years.

I remember once when we were in an Indian restaurant and a woman on the next table was being very boring about her dog. She was lecturing her friend on how circuses exploited animals by training them to do tricks. Then she went on to say that nonetheless her own dog could perform several tricks which he had taught himself.

Diz couldn't restrain himself any longer. He leant over and said, 'Like f—king barking, I suppose'.

George Melly

When I was with the Ken Colyer Band the banjo player was Diz Disley. One day we all travelled to Manchester by train. Disley was late as usual and had to catch the next train. Unfortunately, he didn't have enough money to buy a ticket, so he bought a platform ticket and dodged the ticket collector all the way up from London.

As the train was pulling into Manchester, Disley was leaning out of a window mentally congratulating himself on how he'd got away with it when the ticket collector tapped him on the shoulder. Diz jumped back in mock surprise and said, 'You've made me drop my ticket on the track.'

▶ Acker Bilk pictured at the height of the 'Trad Boom' demonstrating that his singing was as popular as his clarinet playing. *In the foreground:* Ron McKay (*drums*) and Colin Smith (*trumpet*).

At the station the ticket collector escorted Disley to the barrier and told them to let him through as he had personally witnessed Diz accidentally drop his ticket out of the window as they were pulling into the station.

Acker Bilk

The story I like about Diz Disley is how he found himself a bit short of money one December, so he took a Christmas job as a temporary postman.

Apparently in the first street on his round he pushed back the letter-box of a front door and heard the sound of Django Reinhardt blasting out, so he rang the bell to congratulate the occupant on his fine choice of records. The chap who came to the door recognised Diz and invited him for a drink and a chat about Django.

Disley spent most of the week in this house and eventually

he took sacks of mail back to the Post Office saying, 'Give it to me next year and I'll try again.'

Digby Fairweather

When I was with the Ted Heath Orchestra around 1946–7, all the saxophone players were expected to double on clarinet. The moment of truth occurred when we made the musical film *London Town*, and all these superb players from the London symphony orchestras were augmented. The clarinet section comprised Reginald Kell, Jack Brymer, myself and Johnnie Gray. I would publicly like to thank Mr Kell and Mr Brymer for never laughing once.

Ronnie Scott

At one time we used to sing the 'Whiffenpoof Song', with me, Tony Coe and Joe Temperley singing close harmony around one microphone. Unfortunately, Joe and Tony were heavily into Indian food at the time and after about four bars I began to lapse into unconsciousness.

Humphrey Lyttelton

Vic Lewis and I used to play together in a band led by Buddy Featherstonhaugh when we were in the RAF during the war. Vic had heard about these new electric guitars so he got an RAF electrician to make him one with a foot-switch from an old sewing machine.

He persuaded Buddy to let him use it on our next recording session. The first tune that Vic had a solo on, he pushed down the switch, and flash ... he looked like one of those zany cartoon characters who have just been blown up.

Jack Parnell

The drummer Pete Appleby was the epitome of a South Londoner. Apart from believing that life stopped at the River Thames, he was always boasting how he'd just stitched someone up on a second-hand car deal. Also he wore a pork-pie hat when nobody else wore a hat at all.

He had this fantasy that all the chicks, as he would call them, said he looked like Frank Sinatra. This was in the late 1950s when, in reality, he looked more like the Sinatra of today.

He told us that during the war he had served in the Royal Navy on a ship commanded by the Duke of Edinburgh; he would say, 'Me and Phil used to do everything together.'

George Melly

The first time I went to San Francisco with Stephane Grappelli we were entertained at George Shearing's house. Of course, Stephane and George played together at Hatchett's in Piccadilly throughout the wartime blitz. Apparently, when the band emerged into the blackout after the job, they would all hold onto each others' coats and walk along in a line with George in front because, being blind, he was the only one who knew where to go.

Diz Disley

I remember that because I worked at Hatchett's; it was a dinner/dance club. One night I arrived a bit early so I could get a drink before we started. I walked into the bandroom, switched on the light and put my trumpet case on the table. All of a sudden a voice behind me said, 'Hello, Kenny, how are you?' It was George Shearing in the corner reading a braille book.

Another nice story is how George was standing by some traffic lights when a bloke tapped him on the arm and asked him if he would take him across the street because he was blind. So George took him across.

Kenny Baker

Freddy Grant was clarinettist and co-leader of my Paseo Band in the early 1950s and a health freak. We always wondered why he turned up at gigs with a carrier bag full of pink tubing. It turned out that he had a side-line as a specialist in colonic irrigations.

Humphrey Lyttelton

A 1945 session at Feldman's, 100 Oxford Street, London W.1. Pete Chilver (*guitar*); Bob Burns (*tenor sax*); Jack Fallon (*bass*); Kenny Baker (*trumpet*); Jock Bain (*trombone*); Tommy Pollard (*piano*); Eric Delaney (*bongoes*). The obscured drummer is probably Norman Burns.

There is a story of an event many years ago in Studio 51 on a night when Jimmy Skidmore was leading the group. Studio 51 was a long, narrow basement club with the stage at one end and the toilets at the other. It used to get so full that you physically could not get from the stage to the toilets on some occasions.

On this particular night Dill Jones was on piano. During the first intermission he went across the street to the Porcupine pub for a drink and he meets one of our leading piano and vibraphone players who happens to be free that night and is enjoying a skinful of beer. Anyway, Dill manages to convince this pianist, who shall remain nameless, to play the second set for him, with Dill returning for the last set.

The switch is made, but after two or three numbers the dep pianist has the uncontrollable urge to throw up. He realised he would never make it to the toilets, so he looked around to see if anybody was actually watching him and decided to chance it. He stood up and was sick over the 'dark side' of the piano and then carried on playing.

Nobody noticed anything and at the end of the set he apologised to Jimmy Skidmore about being sick half-way through 'Night and Day'. Jim told him not to worry, it often made him feel sick.

Alan Elsdon

The only cricketer I can think of from the late 1920s is Maurice Allom, who played saxophone with Fred Elizalde and his Cambridge Undergraduates orchestra.

Actually, people think I am not much of a sportsman, but when I was at Eton I was a deadly fast bowler. In fact one day, when I was running up to bowl, the ball flew out of the back of my hand and hit the old man who used to walk around the boundary selling sweets. It broke his knee.

Humphrey Lyttelton

Actually, Maurice Allom took a hat-trick bowling for England in a Test match. I can't think of any other saxophone player who has done that.

Benny Green

As you know, I am a member of the MCC. Well, one day last year, I took Harry Gold along to Lord's to watch the cricket. He was so impressed he enquired how he could become a member. As he was seventy-eight years old at the time I thought it was only fair to point out that there was a ten-year waiting list. 'That's all right', he replied.

John Barnes

John Barnes once told me that his idea of paradise would be sitting on the steps of a cricket pavilion watching a match with a cat in his lap and a stack of Duke Ellington records inside for after stumps were drawn.

Peter Clayton

One night when the Ted Heath Band were sharing the bill with another big band, Johnny Hawksworth was coming off stage carrying his bass. As he passed the other bass player going on, he leant over and said, 'Watch the bowler at your end.'

Actually Johnny has got a strange hobby. He's been having his photograph taken once a month for over thirty years in those automatic cubicles. He's got them all linked together in a big wad so he can thumb through them and watch himself grow old.

Ronnie Scott

I often play Sunday concerts on a stage which has been set for some dramatic production which is going on in the theatre during the other six nights of the week.

On one occasion we were working on a stage covered in papier-mâché rocks which was a *King Lear* set. The bass player was perched on the rock where Lear went mad and I was in the hut.

Another time I played a concert with the Alex Welsh Band at the Royal Festival Hall which was actually recorded. On that occasion the stage was set for *Where the Rainbow Ends*, and I was able to make my humble entrance through a large Victorian fireplace.

George Melly

Years ago when I was in the Sandy Brown Band I remember playing in the British Legion Hall, Harrow, one night. During the intermission Sandy and I went across the road for a drink in this little pub run by two dear old ladies. I asked for a sweet Martini and this little old girl put a half-pint mug on the bar and started searching for the correct bottle.

As soon as Sandy saw the size of glass she intended serving he decided to have one as well. Anyway, she eventually produced this dusty old bottle, which hadn't been disturbed for many a year, and poured us two half-pints for six pence each. We couldn't believe our luck and naturally we told the rest of the band.

The next time we played at Harrow the band had an early pick-up so we could have a sweet Martini or two before we started. Unfortunately, she produced six miserable little glasses and charged us half a crown each. I suppose she discovered the correct price when she bought some new stock.

Diz Disley

I remember seeing The Alberts [Len and Duggie Gray] do an act where one of them asked the other if he would like to go for the 64,000-dollar question. When he answered yes, the first brother tipped a bucket of water over the second one and left the bucket covering his head.

After the laughter died down, a muffled voice from under the bucket said, 'Can you repeat the question?'

Ronnie Scott

Bruce Lacey used to work with The Alberts; he played an amplified penny farthing bicycle with a rubber bone.

He gave me a lift home one night in his van and we got stopped by the police. When they asked him what he'd got in the back, he told them there were three skeletons, a tin bath, a few rockets and an amplified penny farthing bicycle. They had a look, and it was absolutely true.

Acker Bilk

I worked for many years with Pat Halcox when we were together in the Chris Barber Band and I must say, although he is a marvellous trumpet player, he is the world's worst teller of jokes – he always forgets the punchlines.

At that time Chris and Ottilie Patterson used to travel separate from the band. So one day we are driving to play a concert in Colchester when we had to slow down for some traffic congestion, which turned out to be a crowd of people surrounding Chris's car which is in a ditch. We could see that Chris was okay because he waved us on ... I think.

When we arrived in Colchester we told the promoter that Chris and Ottilie would be slightly delayed and that we would start without them. Pat said he would take over the announcements, and I remember thinking at the time that I hoped he would make a better job of this than he did telling jokes. After the opening number Pat goes into this great spiel on how we always enjoy playing in Colchester and then starts rambling on about Duke Ellington, finally announcing 'Creole Love Call'. Then he stepped back and played 'Mood Indigo'.

Monty Sunshine

Spike McIntosh played trumpet with the Wally Fawkes Band in the late 1950s.

He was a great fan of Messrs Gordon's and Louis Armstrong. In fact I suspect his real reason for playing trumpet was to capture other musicians and take them home with him in order to drink the product of one and listen to the product of the other.

George Melly

There is a lovely story about Spike McIntosh being at a party at Wally Fawkes's house. In those days Wally had a large divider in his main living room which was covered in pottery, glassware, bowls of fruit and that sort of thing. Typically, Spike was amongst the last to leave and, as he heaved himself out of an armchair, he stumbled into this divider which crashed to the floor with Spike sprawled across the wreckage.

The crash woke up Wally's daughter, then about nine years old. She came out on to the landing in some distress. Prostrate in the middle of the wreckage, Spike saw her at the top of the stairs. With as much dignity as he could muster he said, 'Shouldn't that child be in bed?'

Humphrey Lyttelton

JAZZ GREATS AND
LEGENDARY FIGURES

T he best description I know of early jazz is that it was a form of music popular amongst the working classes in the southern states of the USA.

Jazz theorists argue about the importance and origins of its various component influences but it certainly 'came together' during the period of the First World War, 1914–18, and it was on the move by May 1915 when trombonist Tom Brown took a band of musicians from New Orleans to play Lamb's Café in Chicago. It has always intrigued me how 'New Orleans' musicians became famous in Chicago and 'Chicago' musicians became famous in New York.

Over the last 75 years or so, certain jazz musicians have emerged as 'jazz greats'; by this I mean they were innovators of a particular style of playing which impressed both other musicians and the general public alike.

The most obvious candidate for this description would be Louis Armstrong. He was born in New Orleans in 1900, learnt to play cornet in a Waifs' Home, became the first recognised jazz soloist and by the time he died in 1971 his popularity was such that the whole world knew what a jazz trumpet sounded like.

'Legendary figures' are by definition the subject of much supposition. 'Big Bill' Broonzy, Eddie Condon and Slim Gaillard were all larger-than-life examples. Many of the great jazz musicians and even some of the legendary pioneers have played in Britain since the 1920s and this chapter recalls the stories they told and the memories of the musicians who worked with them.

Sidney Bechet wrote 'Petite Fleur' when he was sharing a flat in Paris with a French drummer known as Moustache. He was actually sitting on the lavatory when he had the idea, so he called out to Moustache to pass his soprano sax in to him.

After a while Bechet emerged feeling more comfortable and equipped with a new tune. Moustache congratulated him on his latest composition and enquired what he was going to call it. Bechet replied, 'Seeing what I was doing at the time, I'll call it "Petite Fleur".'

What nobody appreciates is that the French idiom for a certain bodily function is 'poser des fleurs' – to plant flowers.

Chris Barber

The trouble with Sidney Bechet imitators is that they copy his late period – what I call his French period. During this time his worst characteristics were on display, the over-wide vibrato and so on. Having said that, nobody really sounds like Bechet any more than they sound like Beiderbecke or Armstrong.

Bob Wilber

Sidney Bechet came to Britain in 1919 with Will Marion Cook's Orchestra. A group from the band were summoned to Buckingham Palace to play for King George V.

In his recorded memoirs he said that he expected the Palace to be bigger than an ordinary house, and it was. He said it looked like Grand Central Station, but with carpets hanging on the walls.

Afterwards, he and the other musicians went to a nearby pub. 'That's a funny thing,' he recalled, 'looking at your money to pay for a gin and seeing someone you know.'

Humphrey Lyttelton

Denny Wright [was] playing 'Stardust' with a group one night when a very old Hoagy Carmichael, in the last years of his life, slipped quietly and unannounced onto the piano stool. Somebody in the band turned around and complained about some old guy at the piano who didn't even know the chords.

Digby Fairweather

'I got Rhythm' first appeared in the 1930 stage musical *Girl Crazy*. When you consider that Red Nichols led the pit orchestra, which included Benny Goodman, Glenn Miller, Jack Teagarden, Jimmy Dorsey and Gene Krupa, it is not surprising the tune quickly became a jazz standard.

Benny Green

I remember a night some years ago when Miles Davis descended upon us at the club with his complete entourage – half a dozen barbers, sixty-four lawyers, eighteen girl-friends and a shoe-shine boy. He was well smashed and he sat in the front just grinning.

At that time we had Professor Irwin Corey in cabaret. He was an old comedian of about seventy years who had worked the American jazz clubs all his life and he was a very funny man. At one point he went over to Miles and snatched off his dark glasses and put them on himself, saying 'No wonder you're smiling, everybody looks black.'

Ronnie Scott

There's a story that a young André Previn went to Birdland to see the great Bud Powell. While Previn was sitting there listening to Harry Edison play his set, a man came in, sat next to him and went to sleep.

At the end of the set Harry Edison came over to André Previn and offered to introduce him to Bud Powell. 'It's easy', he said, 'he's asleep next to you.'

Digby Fairweather

I'd always suspected that Big Bill Broonzy had spent a nomadic life living in small rooming houses. My suspicions were confirmed when I arranged for him to stay with my parents when he was appearing in Liverpool. Apparently he was delighted with the spare bedroom, but was troubled because he couldn't find out where to insert the money to make the gas fire work.

George Melly

33

We did a tour in Germany with Big Bill Broonzy. One night, he turned up for the gig with great chunks out of his hair. We thought he had galloping alopecia but, being perfect gentlemen, we didn't make any comment. In the bus on the way to the hall, he started extolling the merits of an electric razor he'd just bought, how it would do this and that. He said, 'You can even cut your hair with it!'

Humphrey Lyttelton

About 10 years ago I had the great honour and pleasure of staying for a week with Billy Butterfield in his home at Fort Lauderdale, Florida.

While I was there he told me of the time when a new club was opening locally. He knew it was backed by gangsters because they approached him to arrange for the Eddie Condon Band to play the opening week and the money was so good that Eddie couldn't possibly refuse.

Anyway, there was a big reception before the club opened to the public and all the band was there except for Eddie Condon. At the last minute a very drunken Condon phoned in to say that he'd met an Irish taxi driver at Miami Airport who had shown him where he could get a drink and he'd join them as soon as he could.

When Eddie arrived, a couple of 'heavies' pulled him out of the taxi, dragged him inside and threw him fully clothed into a cold shower and kept the door shut for 15 minutes. When Eddie emerged he swallowed vast amounts of black coffee, changed into some dry clothes, and didn't touch a drop of alcohol for the rest of the week, which was a great success.

Campbell Burnap

I like the story of Eddie Condon being asked how his band was and he replied: 'Oh, they're fine. They're all sleeping peacefully in their cells.'

Benny Green

Mezz Mezzrow and Eddie Condon faced each other on a radio show in America called *Author meets Critic*. Mezz had just published a book called *Really the Blues* and Condon was the critic.

After a while Condon started criticising Mezzrow's musical arrangements, at which point the chairman butted in, pointing out that he had heard the musicians all over town were interested in Mezz's arrangements. This was quite true, but what he didn't know was that 'arrangement' was Mezz's code word for a marijuana deal.

Digby Fairweather

I remember when the Avon Cities Jazzband accompanied Mezz Mezzrow many years ago. He gave us a list of tunes he wanted to play but we didn't recognise anything at all, which was not surprising as he informed us they were all his originals.

However, the rehearsal turned out very easy because all the tunes were standards like 'Honeysuckle Rose', 'Blue Turning Grey' and 'Christopher Columbus' with different titles.

Geoff Nichols

Frankie Trumbauer was the only true exponent of the C-melody saxophone, and, as I have just done the music for this new film about Bix Beiderbecke where I had to impersonate Trumbauer, I know why the instrument died. It is the most awkward saxophone to play; it is like walking on eggs because one false move and you go totally out of tune. Having said that, Frankie Trumbauer had this wonderful, wispy sound. For me, he was the first 'cool' saxophone player and his style naturally leads you to Lester Young, Stan Getz, Lee Konitz and so on.

It is a strange instrument to hold. At a quick glance it looks like a tenor sax, but you can't hold it beside your body and you can't hold it in front of you. You end up by holding it up in the air, and as I was doing just this, it occurred to me – Lester Young. Now, he started out on C-melody sax and that's how he got his playing stance. Of course by 1930 it was completely obsolete so we have no records of him on the instrument.

Bob Wilber

Did you know I wrote one bar of Duke Ellington's 'Satin Doll'? If you listen carefully to the lyric, you'll hear 'switcheroonie'; that's my bar.

Slim Gaillard

I recently did a tour with one of life's genuine eccentrics, Slim Gaillard. We did a concert in Norwich after which we all went for an Indian meal. Afterwards, Slim said that he was off to the Continent, and the rest of us went back to the hotel. If you tour with Slim Gaillard you get used to him disappearing between gigs.

Next morning I got a message from Slim, allegedly in Paris, to say that he thought he'd left his overcoat in the restaurant and would I pick it up for him. He was worried because there was something valuable in the pocket. I assumed that this was the expensive radio telephone which he had been carrying round on the tour.

Anyway, I hung around Norwich till midday, when the restaurant opened, and, sure enough, the coat was there – but with nothing in the pockets except an old bus pass from last year's Nice Jazz Festival and a half-eaten bag of crisps.

In Birmingham that night, I gave him the coat. He put his hand in the pocket and pulled out the bag of crisps. 'Man, that's great,' he said. 'They're still there!'

Humphrey Lyttelton

It is a tragic loss to the jazz world now that Slim Gaillard has passed on. The last time I saw him was sitting in this very chair in the 100 Club doing a *Jazz Score* broadcast.

Diz Disley

I think Chick Webb was the first drummer, even before Krupa, to bring jazz drumming to the notice of the general public. I used to see him at the Savoy Ballroom in Harlem around 1936/37, and he was a great inspiration to me as he was to every jazz drummer. He was a genius for the time.

Buddy Rich

▶ Bulee 'Slim' Gaillard 1916–91. One of the most eccentric and joyful jazz entertainers. He appeared in several Hollywood movies in the 1940s and wrote many songs featuring his own surreal jive talk.

This was one of the last stories to come back from the States about Buddy Rich.

My colleague, Brian Theobald, was visiting Buddy in hospital just a few days before he died, and he heard a pretty nurse ask Buddy if he was comfortable and was anything bothering him. 'There certainly is something bothering me,' said Buddy in his scalding tone.

37

'What's that, Mr Rich?' said the nurse.
'Country music,' replied Buddy.

Ronnie Scott

Charlie Christian was not the first electric guitarist because both Eddie Durham and Al Casey were before him, but he was the fountain-head of inspiration for all guitarists who followed him. He showed the way how to play in a melodic manner just like horns.

Barney Kessel

Coleman Hawkins was known for being vain about his age. He was only sixty-five years old when he died, even if he did look 108. Jazz fans would ask him about the singer Mamie Smith, whom he worked with in the early 1920s, and he'd tell them he'd never heard of her. Another time somebody asked him what year he joined Fletcher Henderson [1924]. 'Oh,' he said, 'about 1950.'

Humphrey Lyttelton

I think 'Stealin' Apples' is one of the nine tunes which Fats Waller sold to Fletcher Henderson for the price of a bagful of hamburgers.

Humphrey Lyttelton

Around 1929, Fats Waller is alleged to have sold thirty tunes for 500 dollars, and they included 'Ain't Misbehavin'' and 'Honeysuckle Rose'. He needed the money for drink, plus he was continually behind with his alimony payments.

Furthermore, if you read the Fats Waller biographies, they hint at the strong possibility that he also wrote 'On the Sunny Side of the Street' but he had to sell it immediately for the need of urgent cash. Maurice, his son, actually writes that it is a Waller composition and nobody really denies it, although it is attributed to Jimmy McHugh.

Peter Clayton

▶ A shot from the 1943 film *Stormy Weather* showing *from L to R:* Alton 'Slim' Moore, Zutty Singleton, Benny Carter, Gene Porter, Slam Stewart (*bass*), and Fats Waller the supreme jazz entertainer.

The first time I met Louis Armstrong properly was at Schipol Airport, Holland, in 1957 when a few of us were sitting together waiting to see Louis off on his flight. I remember he was drinking 'B & B' [brandy and Benedictine].

It was well past midnight and the cleaners were hoovering around us when Louis turned to Velma [Middleton] and told her to fetch some Swiss Kris, the legendary laxative which Armstrong prescribed for just about everybody he spoke to. Velma dutifully disappeared and shortly returned with four packets of Swiss Kris and four glasses of warm water. Louis insisted that I had one.

Later on, having nowhere to travel that day, I decided to go on a little boat trip around the islands on what was the Zuiderzee in those days. While I was on this small open boat, the Swiss Kris started to work. I've never known anything like it. I just gritted my teeth and held on until we landed, when I rushed into the nearest café screaming for a toilet.

► King Louis surrounded by *L to R:* Tommy Dorsey, Bud Freeman, Pops Foster, Eddie Condon, Red Allen and George Wettling.

It was like that all day long – I'll never touch the stuff again as long as I live!

Beryl Bryden

Louis Armstrong loved the music of Guy Lombardo and his Royal Canadians so much that on one occasion he waited long after his own band had finished just so he could sit in with them.

Humphrey Lyttelton

When Louis Armstrong came over in 1956 to play a charity concert at the Royal Festival Hall, I was amongst the crowd of musicians who gathered at Heathrow Airport to welcome him. You wouldn't believe the twit from BBC Television News who interviewed him and asked if they were all his own teeth. 'Yeah,' said Louis, 'I've just paid the last instalment.'

After that Louis borrowed Spike McIntosh's trumpet and asked me to back him as I had the only chord instrument. He played 'Way Down Yonder in New Orleans' and I remember thinking to myself I hope this is in F. Did you know, when you stand behind Louis while he is playing, his ears go up and down with his phrasing?

When he finished, he handed the trumpet back to Spike with the advice that he ought to get the saveloys removed.

Diz Disley

There's a familiar story about Bunk Johnson losing his front teeth, having to give up playing and retiring to the rice-fields of New Iberia – until the day, of course, when he was rediscovered, given new teeth and so on.

In reality, eye-witnesses say that he was playing local gigs all the time. He got over the shortage of teeth by winding twine around his surviving canine teeth and playing with the mouthpiece against that.

Humphrey Lyttelton

Wasn't it Henry Ford who said 'Bunk is History'?

Benny Green

I knew Django Reinhardt. In fact I particularly remember one day before the war when we were both in Leonard Feather's office in Holborn. Leonard was showing us his new home recording unit. You just put the needle onto the wax, and when it was finished you brushed off the excess wax.

Django Reinhardt and I made a swing version of the National Anthem that afternoon.

George Chisholm

Yes, I knew Django, but of course I've worked much more with Stephane [Grappelli]. In fact Stephane has told me so much about Django that I expect I know more about Django than I do about Stephane. He used to say, 'That Django, I love 'im, but sometimes I 'ate 'im. He was a gypsy you know. That was not the reason, but sometimes 'ee was not too clean. 'Is feet, that was something to 'ear.'

Alan Clare

Stephane Grappelli told me that Django Reinhardt couldn't read or write, but he would always tag along with Stephane to business meetings which concerned the Hot Club of France. Apparently he would sit there pretending he could understand what was going on until he felt he ought to make his presence felt. At this point he would grab the contract from Stephane and point to a paragraph at random and say, 'Non, non.'

Invariably it would be the clause which said the band were guaranteed free accommodation and food.

Humphrey Lyttelton

I was commissioned to collect Stephane Grappelli very early one morning for a recording session – you can guess who paid the taxi fare. Actually, my group backed him for ten years, during which time he bought two rounds of drinks. One of those occasions we have on photograph because my bass player, Phil Bates, was so amazed he took out his camera and captured this historic event on film.

Anyway, we got to the studios about 9.30 am and the doorman directed us to a large sound stage as yet only dimly lit. I told Stephane to get his violin out and make himself comfortable while I tried to find us a couple of cups of tea.

On my way out of the studio I noticed a figure down at the dark end of the room. As I approached this figure I realised it was a man standing on his head with his feet against the wall, and I recognised him as Yehudi Menuhin. Now, I am not sure what the procedure is for talking to a man standing on his head, so I assumed this Quasimodo-like posture. I wished him

▶ Duke Ellington with Django Reinhardt 'The most creative jazz musician to originate outside the USA' according to Duke's son Mercer.

good morning and explained I was getting some hot drinks and would he like anything. 'Yes,' he said, 'a hot chocolate would be admirable.'

That was the first time I met Sir Yehudi Menuhin.

Diz Disley

There's a wonderful story about Baby Dodds many years ago making a 78 rpm record where he talks and musically demonstrates how to play jazz drums. The story goes that he started off by saying, 'First you hold the sticks like this.'

Campbell Burnap

There's a story behind the Thomas 'Fats' Waller recording of 'St Louis Blues'. It was booked as a duet for Waller and Jelly Roll Morton, but Morton didn't show up. Waller went out into the street looking for Jelly Roll in the local bars and he found Bennie Payne, later to become Billy Daniels's pianist and musical director.

Waller is alleged to have said, 'Hey, kid, do you want to make some quick money?'

They went back to the studio together and recorded 'St Louis Blues'.

Peter Clayton

I like the story Earl Hines told of the days when he was with Louis Armstrong at the Sunset Café in Chicago in the late 1920s. Through the night, the band used to play everything, including the dance set and backing the cabaret. For the very last set, musicians used to drop by to sit in, and anyone who'd written a new number would bring it along and get the band to run it through. Some of the visiting musicians weren't too hot at reading.

One night Fats Waller came by with one of his new songs. He handed out the parts, climbed up to the piano which was on a high rostrum and beat in the number. Halfway through, he leant over and shouted, 'What key are you guys struggling in?'

Humphrey Lyttelton

My band was playing at the Cork Festival a couple of years back when Tony Bagot, my bass player, ran into Benny Waters. They knew each other from years earlier in Germany.

When it got around to Benny asking Tony who he was playing for these days and he found out it was me, he said, 'Shit. Is he still alive?'

Monty Sunshine

I played alongside Benny Waters quite recently at the Edinburgh Festival; it really is a traumatic experience. You climb onto the bandstand with half a hangover, convinced you've got the flu coming, and all of a sudden this man in his middle eighties starts roaring the life out of any reed instrument he cares to pick up.

John Barnes

I think the circumstances when Charlie Parker played tenor sax were very similar to when I worked with Sonny Stitt in Chicago during my college days. Stitt's alto sax was often in the pawnshop, so he would use the tenor sax which the club management kept behind the bar for emergencies.

Don Lanphere

I remember compering a BBC TV outside broadcast from Reading University which featured Sonny Rollins. Terry Henebery, the producer, had set everything up and told me I could start announcing the rhythm section while he quickly retired to the control wagon outside. However, no sooner had I started announcing the rhythm section than Sonny Rollins broke into his composition 'St Thomas' from the depths of the bandroom, and emerged playing the tune as he made his way to the bandstand.

In fact, Terry hadn't even reached his controls when Rollins had started. The floor manager appealed to me to stop the music as he was getting panic messages down his headphones, but I decided it would be better to let Rollins finish the tune and Terry could start recording from the next number.

It was a thirty-minute programme and Sonny Rollins played 'St Thomas' for forty-five minutes! Meanwhile Terry Henebery had decided he could use what he'd got as long as he could get the first two or three minutes repeated to use behind the opening titles. I asked Sonny Rollins for the opening two minutes again. He just nodded and played the same tune for another forty-five minutes.

Humphrey Lyttelton

When Sonny Rollins first played for us, the club was still in Gerrard Street. He was booked for a month with a rhythm section led by Stan Tracey on piano. Anyway, they rehearsed

► Sonny Rollins pictured with the boss at the original Ronnie Scott's in Gerrard Street, Soho. He declined the offer of an early breakfast.

for four hours on the afternoon they were due to open and during the whole month they didn't play anything they had rehearsed.

He was a strange guy in many ways. Every night he insisted on walking back to his hotel dressed in his black hat and long black overcoat. I was getting into a taxi with Allan Ganley one night as Sonny Rollins came out of the club, so I offered to take him with us to an all-night snooker club where he could meet a lot of 'night-people' and have a good breakfast etc. I told him he would see a slice of London life. 'No,' he said, 'but you go ahead and have a nice slice.'

Ronnie Scott

JAZZ MUSICIANS'

HUMOUR

J azz musicians' acerbic, black humour is legendary. It is directed mainly towards their friends, themselves and the music they love. Sharing this humour with a wider audience was one of the main reasons why BBC Radio launched the *Jazz Score* series back in 1981.

If Coleridge Goode, Thad Jones and Dudley Moore formed a group, they could call it 'The Goode, the Thad and the Dudley'.

Ronnie Scott

I've often thought that if Stan Getz and Stuff Smith had ever got together, they could have called the group 'Getz-Stuffed'.

Acker Bilk

Acker, can you identify this American clarinet player who lived in France for many years? Then his circumstances changed – they buried him.

Benny Green

A bandleader I used to work for always announced any Glenn Miller number by saying, 'You know Glenn Miller, he did the music for World War Two.'

Alan Elsdon

I met Carl Baritteau in Melbourne. He said he loved it in Australia, and how hospitable native Australians were. The only drawback was the white people.

Ronnie Scott

As we all know, Wally Fawkes has one of the driest wits in the business. I remember being with Wally and a crowd of other musicians in a pub one day when another well-known musician came over and started crying on our collective shoulders. In fact he was notorious for boring everybody with his domestic problems and personal traumas.

Well, one by one we glazed over and made our excuses for moving elsewhere, except Wally who listened most sympathetically to this diatribe for about half an hour before taking this bloke's arm and saying, 'Would it help to talk about it?'

Ian Christie

There really is a Swedish trumpet player called Bent Persson, but do you remember some of the Scandinavian musicians we used to invent?

There was the rickety Swedish trombonist – Bent Legs; the Danish drummer – Knut Loose; the sexy pianist – Sven Lightsarlo; the drunken sax player – Olaf Awhisky; not forgetting the Country and Western singer – Lars Roundup.

Benny Green and Ronnie Scott

Some ill-informed person actually invited the blind pianist Eddie Thompson to umpire a cricket match. Once when he was telling the story, a joker asked him what he would have done if there'd been an appeal for bad light. Eddie said, 'No problem – I'd have my light meter with me.'

Humphrey Lyttelton

There was a pianist of European extraction called Frecko von Humperdau living in Montreal. Some local musicians spotted his telephone number in the Musicians' Directory and decided to play a joke on him.

One of them phoned him up and pretended to book him to play for a major film production. Astronomic figures were discussed about the fee and various aspects of the music considered. Well, this pianist couldn't believe his luck and he was agreeing to all sorts of outlandish suggestions.

As the conversation drew to a close, the 'booker' told him he looked forward to meeting him with his bass trombone at the studios. 'Bass trombone', says Frecko, 'I play piano.'

'Sorry', said the booker, 'I must have got the wrong Frecko von Humperdau.'

Alan Elsdon

Roses are red, violets are blue,
I'm schizophrenic, and so am I.

Benny Green

I only know two left-handed trombonists. One is my Uncle Hymie, who had his right arm stolen after an accident. The other is Slide Hampton, if you'll excuse the expression.

Ronnie Scott

A few months ago we had the American saxophone player Teddy Edwards here in the club on a Friday night. We were really jammed; there was lots of dancing and a really great ambience.

I was standing at the bar with my partner Ted Morton when an old regular came up to Ted and remarked on what a good evening it was and how everybody seemed to be enjoying themselves. 'Yes,' said Ted, 'I suppose there's not much we can do about it now.'

Roger Horton

Did Irving Mills really write the lyrics to some of Duke Ellington's tunes? I always suspect agents who get their names in the credits. In fact, I heard that Duke wrote 'It Don't Mean A Thing If It Ain't Got That Swing' and Mills wrote 'Doo-wah, doo-wah, doo-wah, doo-wah, doo-wah, doo-wah, doo-wah, doo-wah.'

Humphrey Lyttelton

I like the story of the two American musicians walking along a street when they see a newspaper billboard claiming 'Indiana Bridge Disaster'. One turns to the other and remarks, 'Indiana hasn't got a bridge, has it?'

Digby Fairweather

I remember seeing George Chisholm with the Teddy Joyce Band. In fact, even earlier, I remember seeing Teddy Joyce at the Trocadero, Elephant and Castle [district of South London].

I used to go there as a youngster. Me and my cousin Knocker would get free tickets from the fish shop because they displayed a poster of coming attractions. On a Friday night they had a big show with at least five acts and a film.

Once in a while one of the acts would get the 'bird'. Now, when you got the 'bird' at the Trocadero they really meant it – you could hear the raspberries and booing half-way down the Walworth Road. The crowd would start shouting, 'Bring on Rasher.' Now, Rasher was a character who sold tips on greyhound winners in the foyer. So the manager would find Rasher and send him on stage. He'd sing two choruses of 'Mother, I Love You', everything would go quiet and the show could continue.

George Webb

Our next guest is a man who claims to have lost £5 the last time he played here at 100 Oxford Street. So, if anyone finds a white £5 note will they please return it to – George Webb.

Benny Green

I try to forget those records which I made with Humphrey Lyttelton in the late 1940s because, even to this day, I meet people who ask me for their money back.

George Webb

The drummer Jake Hanna has a lovely sardonic sense of humour. He always maintains that Glenn Miller should have lived and his music should have died.

Ronnie Scott

Over the years people have made fun of Glenn Miller's arrangements, but actually, if you think about it, his music is much
better than it sounds.

Barney Kessel

Do you know the difference between a banjo and a trampoline?
You take your shoes off before you jump on a trampoline.

Acker Bilk

Do you know the difference between a ukulele and a banjo? A
banjo takes longer to burn?

Campbell Burnap

There's a very famous album called 'The Buck Clayton Jam
Session'. Bruce Turner always refers to it as 'The Jack Clayton
Bum Session'.

Digby Fairweather

Bruce Turner always refers to clarinet players Jimmy Noone
and Omer Simeon as Jimmy No one and Omer Someone.

Humphrey Lyttelton

Bruce Turner has been calling everybody 'Dad' for so long
now that he doesn't know what to call his father.

George Melly

The latest Bruce Turner story I have heard is how he went up
North to play a guest spot with a local 6-piece jazzband who
specialised in novelty-type jazz. Their big number was the
complete Pee Wee Hunt version of '12th Street Rag' including
the 'Doo-Whacka-Doo' muted trumpet solo.

At the end of the number Bruce went across to the trumpet
player and said: 'Dad, dad. Don't whacka-doo, don't whacka-
doo'.

Digby Fairweather

I've spent a lot of time working in Germany over the years. I
remember sitting in a café in Cologne one day when I got into
conversation with this older German jazz fan.

Eventually, he got around to telling me that Field Marshal
Rommel was a jazz fan. When I queried how he knew that,

he told me that he had spent two years in North Africa with Rommel during the war and it was well known that in the middle of the night he would wake up and shout out, 'Where's Montgomery?'

Ronnie Scott

Eddie Thompson was a beautiful guy and a great pianist. Apart from that he had an amazing talent for scrambling song titles. So you would get tunes like 'I Water the Front Cover', 'Bike up the Strand', 'I Won't Chance a Stand with a Ghost Like You', or he'd announce that lovely ballad from Jerome Kern called 'The Night You Looked Away'.

Benny Green

Stan Getz is a truly marvellous saxophone player and I have been an admirer of his for longer than I can remember, but he is definitely no shrinking violet. In fact, he has an ego like the side of a house.

It so happened that one of his visits to the club coincided with my contracting a very bad back. I told everybody that I got a slipped disc by bending over backwards to please Stan Getz.

Soon afterwards I was on tour with my group and we used to pass the time away by planning tunes that Getz could use on his next album – 'All the Things I Am', 'I Am Your Heart's Delight', 'There Will Never be Another Me' and so on.

Ronnie Scott

I visited an Italian restaurant in New York which was run by the Mafia. The house speciality was broken leg of lamb.

Ronnie Scott

You know clarinet players sometimes hold their reed against a coin and burn the top edge away to harden them? Well, a certain clarinet player turned to the pianist Bert Murray and asked if he'd got a 10p piece to burn his reed and Bert looked

► George Chisholm was Britain's No. 1 trombone player for decades after his arrival in London in 1936. He broke into his honeymoon in 1938 to record with Fats Waller and has been 'first call' ever since.

up, saying, 'Here's a quid, burn the whole bloody clarinet.'

Alan Elsdon

That was Barney Kessel playing with Stephane Grappelli. We've been great friends for years and he is a wonderful guitarist. He just gets that one diminished wrong – but then he always does. What the hell.

Herb Ellis

You're asking me whether it is true or false that Ella Fitzgerald appeared in a Bing Crosby film with her uncle Barry Fitzgerald! Come off it, Ella Fitzgerald is Irish, isn't she?

Acker Bilk

Do you remember the Sammy Kaye Band had the motto 'Swing and Sway with Sammy Kaye'? Some of us thought up the motto 'Swing and Sweat with Charlie Barnet'.

Ronnie Scott

'I Want a Little Girl', a lovely song. It certainly wasn't Roman Polanski singing it. I should say that was Jimmy Rushing.

George Melly

Didn't somebody say about Polanski 'I wouldn't touch him with a five-foot pole'?

Benny Green

Did you hear the story about the great jazz fan who died a little while ago? He was quite rich and used to follow several bands around. He would take them out for meals and buy everybody drinks and all that sort of thing.

Well, when he died there were lots of jazzers who turned up at his funeral. There were jazz records played in the chapel. It was all very moving, except that, just as the coffin slid through the curtains for the cremation, Count Basie's version of 'April in Paris' finished, and as Basie said, 'One more time', the coffin started coming back through the curtains.

Acker Bilk

Ian Christie was responsible for some great put-downs. I remember when a certain well-known personality on the British jazz scene confessed to being paranoiac. Ian told him, 'No, you've got it wrong. Paranoia is when you *think* people don't like you.'

Humphrey Lyttelton

► 'I've just heard from Bill Bailey and he ain't coming home' – a typical remark from James Moody in the middle of a raving solo.

James Moody has worked the club several times. He has a great line in patter. In the middle of a raving solo he will break off and announce, 'I've just heard from Bill Bailey and he ain't coming home', and then carry on playing.

Ronnie Scott

I saw James Moody at the Cork Jazz Festival quite recently. He said, 'I'm going to play, "I Can't Get Started",' and played one note.

George Melly

I had an uncle who wrote '9th Street Rag', '10th Street Rag' and '11th Street Rag'; then he died.

Ronnie Scott

► A typical *Jazz Score* cast looking forward to a well earned drink after a live recording at the Prince of Orange, Rotherhithe, SE London. *L to R:* Ronnie Scott, Acker Bilk, Benny Green, Humphrey Lyttelton and George Melly.

I had an uncle who had a lot of bad luck as a composer. Actually, he had a lot of near misses like 'Seventy Four Trombones' and then he almost had a hit with 'Trouble over Bridgwater'.

Acker Bilk

When I used to sing 'Miss Jenny's Ball', Mick Mulligan would announce that I was going to sing a song concerning a 'uni-testicular' lady.

George Melly

When the BBC broadcast the news of the death of the jazz musician Bennie Green, the American trombone player, several people phoned me up to see how I felt.

Benny Green

Bob Dawbarn was the trombonist with the Mick Mulligan Band when I first joined them. His raincoat was so filthy, he made those fellows who go into live sex shows in Soho look positively spruce.

George Melly

Zoot Sims was one of the dearest and funniest guys I know. I remember when we were sitting together in my office watching TV the night the Americans landed on the moon. As we watched these guys floating around, Zoot turned to me and said, 'Look at that, they're walking on the moon and I'm still playing "Indiana".'

Ronnie Scott

We stayed in a small hotel the other night run by a Belgian couple. Talk about mean, he turned the gas off while she turned the bacon over and when we went in to breakfast we found the tomato ketchup on an optic.

Acker Bilk

Who was it who said of Woody Herman, 'There, but for the grace of Ralph Burns, goes Ted Lewis.'

Campbell Burnap

His mother was a titled lady – she was the Southern Area Light-Heavyweight Champion.

Ronnie Scott

My favourite violin story is about the really broken-down tramp who goes into this very smart music house in Bond Street and puts this battered violin case on the counter and offers it for sale. The assistant opens up the case and decides he needs a second opinion, so he takes it to their expert violin maker in the back room.

Anyway, it turns out to be Stradivarius worth about £300,000, so the assistant offers the tramp £50. The tramp hesitates, so the offer is upped to £100. The tramp is still not sure, so the assistant asks what price he had in mind. 'About £280,000,' said the tramp.

Ronnie Scott

I like Jack Benny's story of how his violin used to belong to his great grandfather, who gave it to his grandfather, who gave it to his father, who *sold* it to him.

Benny Green

There is a story that at the funeral of bandleader Alex Welsh, John Barnes had to be physically restrained because, as the coffin started to slide through the curtain, he was trying to attach a Musicians' Union sticker which said 'Keep Music Live' onto the coffin.

Campbell Burnap

For a long time Cy Touff played bass trumpet in the Herman Band. I remember going to a Woody Herman concert soon after he had left the band, and when the trumpet section stood up in 'Caldonia' a cockney friend turned to me and said, 'They've got a Touff missing.'

Ronnie Scott

I heard a story about an American comedian who came over to play the London Palladium soon after the war and on the first night he died an absolute death.

When he got backstage Val Parnell was waiting for him with the news that he was finished. Val Parnell told him to listen to the booing front of house. 'They're not all booing', said the comedian, 'some of them are applauding.' 'Applauding', said Parnell, 'those people are clapping the booing.'

Alan Elsdon

We had the American jazz comedian Professor Irwin Corey at the club the same time as the Cedar Walton group. The prof would announce, 'I'd now like to hand you back to the Waltons. Each man is a soloist in his own right – it's only when they play together they get into trouble.'

Ronnie Scott

AMERICAN MUSICIANS IN EUROPE

The first American jazz band to tour Britain was the Original Dixieland Jazz Band in 1919. Their tour was an immediate success and 5,800 people paid to see them when they played at the opening night of the Hammersmith Palais.

Ever since that time American jazz artistes have been coming over, although there was a fallow period from the mid-1930s until the mid-1950s when the British Musicians' Union barred bands from working here (see p 13).

Nonetheless a few renowned musicians did slip through the net in the late 1930s disguised as 'Variety artistes' e.g. Art Tatum. Benny Carter became staff arranger for Henry Hall's BBC Dance Orchestra in 1936. Coleman Hawkins worked in Jack Hylton's Orchestra at the London Palladium and a couple of years later a very young Dizzy Gillespie also played the Palladium as a member of the complete Teddy Hill Orchestra in the 'Cotton Club Show'. Naturally, during World War Two the rules were relaxed and many jazz musicians came over as members of Glenn Miller's 'Army' Band and Sam Donahue's 'Navy' Band.

In January 1957 the Eddie Condon Band arrived here in exchange for the Ronnie Scott Sextet. The ban was over and British jazz fans were almost overwhelmed as American bands of every style soon arrived here. From Count Basie and Dave Brubeck to Kid Ory and George Lewis.

I remember one night, or I should say one morning, when Pete King and I were helping Ben Webster out of the club because he'd had a little too much to drink. In fact, Ben was unintelligible except for a brief moment of clarity which overcame him as we passed an exceptionally beautiful waitress who was still clearing up. 'Look at the bust on that child', he said, and then he slumped into our arms again.

Ronnie Scott

Ben Webster was once escorted down the stairs by two young policemen after an unruly session at the Dancing Slipper Club in Nottingham. Halfway down, he turned to one of them and asked, 'Did you know Art Tatum?'

Humphrey Lyttelton

A friend of mine, who was learning to play trombone, went backstage to meet Kid Ory during his tour over here in the late 1950s. Anyway, having tracked the great man down in his dressing room, he asked if he had any tips for a young trombonist. 'Sure', said Ory. 'Never play the trombone for nothing.'

Digby Fairweather

I played in the British band which supported the Kid Ory Band on that tour. Henry 'Red' Allen was on trumpet and a funny thing happened with him backstage when he appeared at the Odeon, Hammersmith.

My wife was looking for me amongst the labyrinth of passages at the back of the theatre and eventually in desperation she shouted out, 'Alan.' Immediately a door opened beside her and Henry Allen said, 'Yes, Ma'am, I'm just coming!'

Alan Elsdon

My old room-mate Tony Scott told me about when he was playing clarinet with Romano Mussolini in Rome. Incidentally, Il Duce's son is a damned fine pianist. Anyway, one night a certain American trumpet player, who was never too bright

L to R: Buck Clayton, Beryl Bryden, 'Big Joe' Turner (seated) and drummer Johnny Butts, his wife and Joe Temperley (standing)

up top, walked into the club, went straight over to the piano and said, 'Say, I'm sorry about your old man.'

Mundell Lowe

I met Tony Scott, who was playing his clarinet in that rather fearsome style of his, at a festival weekend in Holland.

We had sprung a leak in the radiator of our bandwagon and somebody had come up with the bright idea of plugging the hole with chewing gum. Tony Scott came up to us while all the band were crowded around our wagon chewing with great determination. He thought it was some new 'experience' because he asked if he could join in.

George Melly

Wingy Manone toured with my band. I must admit it was quite a gruelling tour; in fact, Wingy spent most of the time asleep in his ancient and voluminous overcoat. One day we were driving to a job in Chester and he woke up just as we were arriving. Looking out of a window, he saw a sign for

61

Chester Zoo and, groaning, he said in disbelief, 'Chester 200 miles'.

Alan Elsdon

I remember Milt Buckner very well. You know he is a rather portly man; well, he's the only person I have seen who can hold his arms behind his back and play the organ with his belly.

Ronnie Scott

I worked quite a lot with Benny Carter just before the war. He always maintained his favourite trumpet player was Bill Coleman.

George Chisholm

I played with the Stan Kenton Orchestra on a couple of occasions when they were on tour over here. The first time he called out 'Peanut Vendor', I couldn't find the music, but the alto player Lennie Niehaus told me not to bother as it was a head arrangement. All I had to do was play bottom B and, when he nudged me, to change to C sharp. It worked out fine.

Benny Green

I was one of a great crowd of musicians who greeted George Lewis and his band of New Orleans musicians on their first visit to London. We met them at one of the stations and I overheard a lovely exchange between British trombonist Peter Dyer, who greeted Jim Robinson in his rather upper-class accent by saying, 'Welcome to the British Isles, Jim,' and Robinson, who grunted, 'Yeah, man, and the same to you.'

Acker Bilk

I'll always remember Bill Evans because his was the very first American group we booked into the club. That was in the old days in Gerrard Street.

We were all terrifically excited at the prospect of an American pianist playing the club and we thought the least we could do was to get a decent piano. So the Saturday morning before he arrived we sold our old piano with the intention of hiring

▶ Bill Evans' was the first American group to play at Ronnie Scott's when he nearly had to play on a small upright piano for 'Mr Evans to see his boys over the top'. This would have appalled Bill Evans who was one of the most sensitive and influential post-war pianists.

a grand piano from a bloke around the corner. When he found out his piano was destined for a jazz cellar, he just refused to have anything to do with us.

Then we tried Steinways and, believe it or not, they didn't have a grand piano in stock. I'll never forget the German lady in charge of rentals at Steinways as she tried to convince us that a small upright piano would be ideal because 'Mr Evans could see the boys over the top.'

Eventually, Alan Clare came to the rescue with a friend's piano.

Ronnie Scott

I'll never forget when the Avon Cities Jazzband accompanied Don Byas on a short tour. His reputation for being a rather fierce man who was rumoured to carry a knife was well known to us, so when he selected me as his regular arm-wrestling partner I made sure he won every night.

Geoff Nichols

I hosted an ill-fated television programme from the London School of Economics which featured the avant-garde American brothers Albert and Don Ayler.

The first problem was their flight arrived late into Heathrow, which put everything behind schedule. The second thing was that Don Ayler disappeared off to the students' canteen because he was starving hungry. After about forty-five minutes the catering manager phoned us and complained that there was an American musician standing on his head at the front of the queue in the canteen and nobody could get served. Apparently, Don Ayler was going through his yoga routine before playing.

Humphrey Lyttelton

I was at the reception in a Soho restaurant when the Eddie Condon Band first came over here. I was with the Chris Barber Band at the time and we had to play a concert that evening in the Recital Room at the Royal Festival Hall. Most of us were rather the worse for wear from drink, and Pat Halcox didn't even turn up at all. By some chance Wild Bill Davison did turn up, so he played with us instead.

Monty Sunshine

I'll never forget the night Thelonious Monk walked into the club when Ornette Coleman was playing his violin. Monk

▶ Controversial saxophone player Ornette Coleman (above on violin) was once touring with a minstrel show and left stranded in New Orleans.

couldn't stand that kind of bullshit and I remember him having a go at Ornette and telling him, 'For God's sake, if you want a violinist in the band, why don't you hire somebody who can play the instrument?'

Ronnie Scott

65

I met Doc Cheatham at the Edinburgh Festival recently. I never knew he was a cousin of Ornette Coleman. In fact, they hoped to make a record together.

Humphrey Lyttelton

Dickie Hawdon is a wonderful trumpet player who was Director of the Jazz and Popular Music Faculty at Leeds College of Music until recently. He is also a very competent double bass player and I was told this story about the time when Dickie was playing bass behind Art Farmer on one of his UK tours.

When Art Farmer passed out the chords for the Thelonious Monk tune 'Round Midnight', Dickie looked at them quizzically remarking that there were some interesting changes. 'I hope so,' said Art, 'I got them from Charlie Parker who got them from Monk.'

Digby Fairweather

I first went on the road at the age of seventeen years with a band led by the Belgian trumpet player Johnny Claes, who lived in London throughout the war.

Johnny had a very small American drummer called Freddy Crump, who was about four feet tall but a terrific showman. His drum feature involved him getting amongst the audience and playing a solo on people's buttons or anything he could find, even on their teeth if he got the chance. The finale of his act was to slide on his backside right across the stage and lean into the orchestra pit and hit the drummer's cymbal on the last chord.

I'll never forget a certain night in Middlesbrough when he misjudged the width of the stage and slid right off and dropped into the middle of the pit.

Ronnie Scott

When Fats Waller visited Britain in 1938 his first job was a week at the Glasgow Empire. He was accompanied by the pit orchestra, which was so unswinging that after the first night he asked them to play him off in 3/4 time.

▶ 'Is that you Mr Armstrong?' Louis being tackled by Max Jones (beret and glasses) at London Airport in 1949. Looking on are *L to R:* Sinclair Traill, promoter Stan Wilcox and organist Robin Richmond.

He used to finish his act by going off doing a sort of Charleston dance, and that was the only way he could detect any sort of beat.

Max Jones

I was backing the ex-Fats Waller guitarist Al Casey in Buxton recently. At the end a chap came up and told us how much he

67

had enjoyed the evening but he'd enjoyed the previous week even more.

Al looked a bit offended, so I quickly asked who had been playing there the previous week and he told us that he couldn't remember the band, but they had pie and mushy peas during the interval.

Alan Elsdon

Did you know that the Blues pianist Speckled Red was really named Rufus Perryman? He was another one I looked after when he toured over here.

I'll never forget his first night, which was on this stage [100 Club]. He was almost blind, poor old bugger, and he spent most of the afternoon working out a programme he laboriously wrote down on a piece of paper which he laid on top of the piano.

Well, in the evening after a couple of numbers whacking the keyboard, the piece of paper dropped inside the piano. We had to half dismantle the piano to find this paper as he didn't know what to play.

George Webb

I played a gig with Yank Lawson a little while back in Cambridge. Yank had come in from Ireland. He was tired, he had toothache and he thought he had a cold coming on, so he wasn't in a very good mood to start with, and I must say the audience were not very appreciative either. Anyway, we decided to leave Yank alone and didn't bother him with conversation.

However, I'll never forget the look on his face at the end of the evening when we were all packing our instruments away in the bandroom, when the door burst open and a young bright-faced jazz enthusiast bounded into the room and made straight for Yank to tell him how marvellous he was and how much he had enjoyed the evening. Then he said, 'I play banjo myself.'

Yank looked up at him slowly and just said, 'Why?'

Campbell Burnap

Yank Lawson has always been a man of few words. This year at the Edinburgh Festival he got involved with a thing called Hornerama which involved about eight trumpet players, many of them screechy high-note guys.

Afterwards, I asked him how he had got on. 'Pretty badly,' he replied. He then thought for a moment and said, 'There were guys up there who were being paid by the note.'

Humphrey Lyttelton

After Eddie 'Lockjaw' Davis had left the Basie band he worked here at the 100 on several occasions. I remember one time asking him what he would like to drink and he ordered a large glass of milk. He went on to explain that he had not been well and how he'd got this bad ulcer and so on. When the milk arrived he slid his hand into his jacket pocket and produced a fifth of Scotch, which he proceeded to tip into the milk as he gave me a great big smile.

Roger Horton

I remember playing in the 100 Club about seven or eight years ago, when Jimmy McPartland sat in with us. Alan Littlejohn was the leader of the band and when he announced Jimmy and mentioned that he had been an original member of the 'Austin High School Gang', a voice boomed out from the back of the club, 'I was at school with you.' A big chap in a rather loud check suit came up to the stage and the pair of them had a really good time that night.

Dick Charlesworth

Bud Freeman sidled up to me in a hotel one day. 'Humphrey, may I ask a personal question – do you have a title?' When I said no, he gave a look as if to say,'Never mind'.

Bud loved England, and it's amazing that after all the touring around doing guest spots in fairly crumby places, he still maintains the elegant and sophisticated air of a rather out-moded English gentleman.

He once bumped into Mick Pyne in Wimbledon High Street

► Edmond Hall, the wonderful clarinet player and enthusiastic Anglophile, getting a morning cup of tea from Peter Clayton.

at 11.30 in the morning. They chatted for a while with the morning shoppers milling around them, and then Bud looked at his watch and said, 'Say, do we have time for cocktails?'

Humphrey Lyttelton

Edmond Hall was another one of those American musicians who was the total Anglophile. Not only did he like Harris tweed and 'county' hats, but he loved cricket as well.

On one occasion, when Ed Hall was over here with Louis

Armstrong's All Stars, he noticed that Louis had been using the hot-iron straightener on his hair. He turned to some of us in the support band and said, 'I see Louis called for the heavy roller this morning.'

Alan Elsdon

Lucky Thompson had this peculiar habit of thoroughly cleaning both his tenor and soprano saxophones after every set and putting them away in their cases. It meant I had to give him twenty minutes' warning every time he was due back on stage.

Ronnie Scott

A little while back I had the privilege of playing some concerts with some great American musicians, because Trummy Young was taken ill and had to fly back to the States. Peanuts Hucko was the leader and the rest of the band were equally as impressive: Billy Butterfield, Marty Napoleon, Gus Johnson and Jack Lesberg.

When I arrived for the first concert I found Peanuts Hucko in the dressing room working out a programme with meticulous care. Anyway, as we came off after the first set I couldn't help wondering what these great American professionals had thought of my contribution. At that moment Peanuts said, 'Well, Campbell, that was just about perfect.' I was thrilled to bits and thanked him profusely. 'I don't mean that,' he said, 'I mean that the set was exactly fifty-five minutes – just what I'd planned.'

Campbell Burnap

Back in the days when I was with Humphrey Lyttelton's band we were playing in a club in Windmill Street one night when I looked up to see Sinclair Traill with this very smartly dressed black man, whom he introduced as Rex Stewart. You can imagine how impressed we were as the Musicians' Union ban had stopped American bands coming over here for years.

Naturally, during the first intermission we all went to the nearest pub to have a drink with this famous American musician. Of course, a JMF [Jazz Man's Friend] came over and stuck his hooter in, as they always do. 'Are you going to have a blow with them?', he demanded. We got rid of him as quickly as possible with a promise of wait and see.

Actually, Rex Stewart did borrow Humph's horn for a blow. While this was going on I noticed the blind pianist Eddie Thompson hanging around, and I suggested that he take over on the piano. Because I was talking to Eddie I only half heard the announcement of the tune they were going to play, so I told Eddie it was 'Indiana'. Well, the cornet intro and the piano playing just didn't seem to be on the same wavelength until Rex Stewart turned to Eddie and said, 'I told you, no piana.'

George Webb

Charlie Mingus worked at the club many times. He was a fearsome bloke – very difficult to deal with and very exacting about his music.

On his third visit he received an income tax demand which really upset him. We told him not to worry and that we would sort it out for him. No, he insisted on going out to the microphone brandishing this brown envelope on every set before his group was in position, and then in stentorian tones he would launch into an admonishment with 'I have just received this letter from your Queen.'

Ronnie Scott

I once did the shortest interview in history with Coleman Hawkins. A BBC producer thought it would be a great idea for me to interview some Jazz stars at the Philharmonic backstage before a concert. So I had to go into the communal dressing-room, with camera man and sound recorder in tow, just as they were getting ready to go on. Eventually I reached Coleman Hawkins, who had been glowering at me from the corner. I said, 'I believe you know a good friend of mine,' and named the person. He said, 'Nope,' and that was it. End of interview.

Humphrey Lyttelton

► 'Very difficult to deal with and very exacting about his music,' is Ronnie Scott's view of bass player/composer Charles Mingus. For sure he became a monster at the sniff of discrimination, real or imaginary.

John Barnes told me of an occasion when he was with the Alex Welsh Band and they were touring with Henry 'Red' Allen. One night they went back to their hotel after a concert and everybody performed their party turn. John did one of his monologues and naturally Lennie Hastings rolled up his trousers and did his impersonation of Richard Tauber.

At the end, they turned to Henry 'Red' and he just sat there and very quietly started singing 'Ol' Man River'. John said it was so moving you could hear a pin drop and the band stood around groping for their handkerchiefs.

Digby Fairweather

I'll never forget Red Kelly. I was in a band which played opposite the Woody Herman Band on a British tour. The deal with the Herman musicians was that they paid their own hotels, and their bass player Red Kelly took great offence at this. So every night he would camp down with anybody who had a bathroom en suite. He would strip off, fill the bath with hot water, get in and go to sleep. When the water got cold, he would let it out, fill up with hot water and go to sleep again. He did this throughout the tour.

Benny Green

It is legendary that Ruby Braff has a prickly disposition. One time when he was working here at the 100, he complained about the rhythm section before the job had started.

During the first intermission I put on a tape of a Woody Herman small group which seemed suitable. I then went to the bar to have a drink with the irreplaceable Sandy Brown, that wonderful clarinet player.

Soon afterwards Ruby joined us and started complaining about the Herman tape. I asked him what was wrong with it and he told me the public didn't like it. I asked him how he knew and he replied he could sense it, and so it went on. Suddenly Sandy Brown looked Ruby Braff straight in the eye and said, 'Ruby, why don't you eat some of those chips instead of stacking them on your shoulder?'

Roger Horton

I heard that somebody wished Ruby Braff a Happy New Year and he turned on them, saying, 'Don't you tell me what sort of New Year to have.'

Ronnie Scott

▶ 'I asked for a piano player and they've given me a disease' is the sort of remark which has given Ruby Braff the reputation of being un-diplomatic. Nonetheless, he is the world's finest cornet player.

I believe there was a conversation which went on in the foyer of this very club [Ronnie Scott's] which involved the American tenor sax star George Coleman and various other musicians.

Anyway, the name of film director Woody Allen came up and somebody was telling how he played New Orleans style clarinet in Michael's Pub in New York once a week. George Coleman was asked if he had seen him. 'Yeah,' he said, 'it was the only time he made me laugh.'

Campbell Burnap

One night my band and Eddie Condon's were invited back to Dr Norman McSwan's house for one of his all-night parties.

These were regular events in Glasgow, at which records were played and large quantities of Scotch consumed, especially on this night. In the early hours of the morning, while Bob Wilber, Wally Fawkes and I were glued to the record-player and enthusing over some solo or other, Eddie Condon lurched over and said, 'Heh, Wilber, quit makin' like a jazz fan.'

Humphrey Lyttelton

Some years back I played in the Cork Jazz Festival with Acker's band and we met the American drummer Barrett Deems on the Aer Lingus flight back to London. Barrett stood in the centre aisle while we were waiting for take off and was giving a running commentary on everything accompanied by clouds of smoke from his pipe.

There were quite a few musicians on the flight apart from Acker's band and we were all loving the show. I remember somebody calling out asking him what he thought of Europe. 'Europe,' he said, 'they should clean it up, paint it and sell it.'

Anyway, when the lights came on for 'No Smoking' and 'Fasten Seat Belts', a hostess came up to Barrett asking him to put out his pipe. At that moment an Irish woman with a very small baby in a shawl tried to squeeze past him. He immediately enveloped this infant in a cloud of smoke, prodded it with his pipe and said, 'Hey, kid, make sure you never get into the music business.' The baby howled all the way to Heathrow.

Campbell Burnap

5

VOCAL ARTISTES

Early jazz singers generally fall into two groups by sex. Males being blues singers accompanying themselves on guitar and females coming from a vaudeville background backed by small groups of musicians. Incidentally, it can be very confusing distinguishing early female singers from each other when listening to scratchy recordings because it seems it was obligatory to be called Smith – Bessie, Clara, Mamie or Trixie.

Later, musicians started to sing, particularly bandleaders e.g. Louis Armstrong, Jack Teagarden and Wingy Manone, but with the advent of big bands and the increasingly sophisticated compositions of the likes of George Gershwin and Cole Porter it was realised that real singers were required. This opened the door for vocalists such as Mildred Bailey, Billie Holiday, Ella Fitzgerald and Lee Wiley.

The main difference between a jazz performance and a 'commercial' rendition by a singer is that in the former the vocal is only a part of the arrangement sharing choruses with the band and musicians' solos, whereas a commercial arrangement is nearly all vocal with just enough instrumental to break up the singing for a few seconds in a three-minute arrangement.

Another difference is that jazz singers become popular for their abilities and not their looks although once in a while the two attributes do come together as in Peggy Lee and Ivie Anderson.

▶ Singer/pianist Nina Simone – fur coat and plastic shopping bag.

Nina Simone has appeared at the club three times so far. The first couple of occasions were like working with a time bomb. The third time was great – I was in Australia.

I remember I was in Perth when the hotel desk rang up to say there was a Mr Pete King on the phone for me from London. I thought how nice it was for him to remember my birthday. When they put him through all I could hear was, 'Help, she's driving me crazy.'

Apparently, Nina Simone would arrive in her chauffeured limousine, stride into the club in her fur coat carrying a supermarket plastic bag, put the bag down by the piano stool, play for ten minutes, pick up her bag and go back to her hotel.

People ask me when we are booking her at the club again. I say it depends on when I can get another tour of Australia.

Ronnie Scott

In his book, Bing Crosby states that the first thing he does in the morning is to play an Eddie Condon record.

Digby Fairweather

Joe Venuti was a very good friend of Bing Crosby. One day when he was visiting the Crosby home he accused Bing of buying cheap furniture. Bing Crosby was indignant at this suggestion, so Joe Venuti pushed his head through all twelve dining chairs.

Benny Green

I always feel nervous when I watch the film *High Society*. When Bing Crosby sings jazzy numbers he always flails his arms about. In the 'Now You Has Jazz' number he comes within a whisker of knocking Louis Armstrong's trumpet down his throat!

Humphrey Lyttelton

That was Rubberlegs Williams singing with Clyde Hart's band around 1945. The reason he sounded rather wild and out of control was because he had just drunk the wrong cup of coffee.

Charlie Parker was in that band and he used to use stimulants. In fact in those days you could buy inhalers for colds which contained strips of benzedrine. Charlie had broken open one of these inhalers and put the benzedrine into his coffee. Unfortunately, Rubberlegs Williams drank Charlie's coffee by mistake and from then on he was flying.

James Moody

I worked with Sacha Distel on TV recently. He played nice guitar, sang well and smelled absolutely adorable.

Ronnie Scott

Betty Smith is not only a booting tenor sax player but she is also a very fine singer.

You know, when Mick Mulligan was in his cups he would turn like a compass to the nearest woman. On one occasion it was Betty Smith. With unusual civility Mick suggested they should commit adultery, to which Betty replied, 'I can't, I'm married.'

George Melly

I have very fond memories of Garland Wilson when he was one of the 'American colony' in Paris around 1953.

One day I was let down by a pianist for a broadcast, so I rushed back to the hotel, which was just around the corner. There were lots of musicians and nightclub people living there, including Garland Wilson. He was still in bed but he immediately agreed to play for me. He put on one of his famous berets, put some trousers over his pyjama bottoms and, leaving his pyjama jacket on, he came back with me to the radio station. We recorded 'I Cover the Waterfront' and a couple of other titles and then he went home to bed again.

Sadly, he died on stage in a Paris nightclub the year after.

Beryl Bryden

You know, Billy Eckstine is a very keen golfer and he always plays when he's over here. One day, he was playing with the bassist Joe Muddel soon after Billy Daniels had been on tour here sporting a most indiscreet toupee. At one hole, Eckstine played a duff shot which dug up an enormous divot. He picked it up, put it on his head and started singing 'That Old Black Magic . . .'.

Humphrey Lyttelton

Ben Webster was a real Jekyll and Hyde where drink was concerned. He was due to play a week at the club but he came a day early so that he could catch the last night of Coleman Hawkins. Well, he's sitting there sinking the booze and having a wonderful time when Billy Eckstine walked in. Immediately, they were all over each other. Naturally, more drinks and much reminiscing until the small hours of the next morning.

The next night Ben came in cold sober and I remarked to him how much he must have enjoyed meeting Bill Eckstine again. 'Billy Eckstine?' he said, 'I haven't seen Billy Eckstine for seven years.' He was dead serious.

Ronnie Scott

Way back in 1950 when I was with the BBC Showband, I remember one of the guests was Frank Sinatra. He brought over his marvellous arrangement of 'Birth of the Blues' with

▶ Frank Sinatra at home with a big band.

its screaming brass passages. Unfortunately for the sound engineers, he insisted on standing in the middle of the brass section because he enjoyed the music so much. They said they couldn't get a balance with him standing there. Sinatra won.

George Chisholm

I should have recognised June Christy's singing; she's a very dear friend of mine. I hope this programme doesn't reach the States or I'll be in trouble.

Herb Ellis

Apparently, Ray Charles Robinson dropped the Robinson from his billing because he didn't want to be confused with the boxer Sugar Ray Robinson, which seems amazing – how could you confuse them?

Benny Green

Big Bill Broonzy had a wonderful selection of malapropisms. He always talked about Fat Wallis for Fats Waller, and Dizzy Gillipsie was another.

He once asked a visiting American musician to pass on a message of best wishes to his English trumpeter friend Kint Cloyer [Ken Colyer].

Humphrey Lyttelton

I did a tour with Brother John Sellars and Big Bill Broonzy together, and very unlikely companions they were, I may add. Broonzy and Brother John didn't get on awfully well together because Broonzy had a rather rugged life-style, while Brother John was rather more delicate in his ways. I can well remember Brother John shaving his head with that depilatory wax which some women use on their legs. This caused a great deal of mockery from Bill.

George Melly

When Blues singer and mouth-organ player Rice Miller 'Sonny Boy' Williamson toured over here with the Chris Barber Band in 1964 he stayed in London with Giorgio Gomelsky.

Even the amazing Giorgio was surprised when Sonny Boy Williamson turned up in the flat with a dead chicken and proceeded to cook it with the feathers on, which covered the flat in thick black dust.

Peter Clayton

I recorded with Josh White once – well, I was in the backing group and Josh White dubbed the vocal on a couple of days later. At one point he sings after I have taken a solo. He was so impressed with my efforts that you can hear him laughing during his vocal. I've still got the record at home.

Benny Green

I was on one of those jazz cruises which sail out of New York. Amongst some wonderful jazz artistes on the ship was Sarah Vaughan. I have been a lifelong admirer of Sarah and we finished up drinking in this little bar very late into the night. We both got rather drunk and I asked her to marry me, but she threw up and went to bed.

Ronnie Scott

Although Joe Williams worked all those years with Count Basie, he actually didn't enjoy singing the Blues; he preferred ballads.

I was at a party where a jazz band was playing and Joe Williams turned up. He was invited to sing a Blues but, pointing to me and Beryl Bryden, he said, 'No, I'll leave it to those two.'

George Melly

My first professional singing job was a residency in Paris in 1953. One night Lionel Hampton came into the club and sat in on drums and piano. I couldn't believe it; my first pro job and I was on the same stage as Lionel Hampton.

Beryl Bryden

83

One of the more extraordinary records which Fats Waller made was 'My Fate is in your Hands' (1929), when he backed the romantic balladeer Gene Austin.

The session came about because Waller had been jailed because he was even further behind in paying alimony than usual. On this occasion none of his friends had the ready cash to bail him out. Gene Austin heard about this and went into court swearing on oath that he needed Fats Waller on a recording session that afternoon.

Peter Clayton

I remember when I led an eight-piece band around 1953–4 we had a singer called Art Baxter. He wasn't the most handsome man in the world, so we used to refer to him as the Singing Pig. Then one day he turned up with an amazing haircut, which I think was self inflicted, so he became the Singing Coconut.

Another time we had a girl singer who didn't quite work out. In fact she was bloody awful, but I was frightened to give her the sack. Her boyfriend was the British Empire Cruiserweight Boxing Champion.

Ronnie Scott

Many years ago Cleo [Laine] and I were working in Holland. After doing a broadcast, some Dutch musicians took us miles away from Amsterdam for a jam session. I told them I would join in for a couple of numbers but Cleo, who hates jam sessions, would just come along for the ride.

Anyway, we arrive at the Hot Sox jazz club, wherever that is, and immediately we hear an announcement which says, 'Ladies and gentlemen. Here they are, that world-famous jazz couple – Cleo Laine and John Dankworth. Take it away Cleo.' Cleo panicked and asked me what she should sing, so quick as a flash I said 'Lady be Good' in C, or 'This Can't be Love' in E flat.

► John Dankworth and Cleo Laine who hates jam sessions.

Right, so I lead the group into a nice eight-bar intro into 'Lady be Good' in C and Cleo comes in with 'This Can't be Love'. There's a story for those critics who think Cleo is too perfect.

John Dankworth

Louis Prima came from New Orleans, and in his early days he played trumpet very much in the style of the other Louis from New Orleans.

I always enjoy his bit in the film *The Jungle Book*. When it first came out my children were of the age when we had to go and see it every holiday. That song he wrote and sang, 'I Wanna Be Like You', was lifted note-for-note from the cornet solo

85

Muggsy Spanier used to play on 'That's a-Plenty'. If you don't believe me, listen to the Bechet–Spanier version, 1940.

Humphrey Lyttelton

Pearl Bailey is a wonderful person with a terrific sense of humour. I remember her particularly from when she was playing a season at the Talk of the Town. She had been seriously ill just before her visit and when she came on stage she described her time in hospital. She pointed out that in America medical treatment is extremely expensive and that you even have to pay for oxygen. 'In fact, for two weeks I couldn't afford to breathe.'

Peter Clayton

In 1955 George Melly was still slim. So slim that on one occasion around that time I shared a hot bath with him. Cheek by jowl, if you know what I mean, not side by side.

Diz Disley

I remember we [Mick Mulligan Band] were somewhat surprised and speculative on learning that we had to back Sister Rosetta Tharpe on a tour; after all, we were not particularly well known for our religious fervour. However, we had nothing to fear. In fact, I used to spend the early part of the evening helping Sister Rosetta demolish a bottle of brandy before she went on.

One evening in Sheffield the press were ushered into her dressing room, so she quickly threw a pair of her knickers over the bottle to 'preserve my image'. Unfortunately her aim wasn't very good so, much to their surprise, they were able to see both items.

George Melly

We did a tour with the Clara Ward Singers, which was quite an eye-opener. I've noticed all these groups of gospel singers have one elderly member who is in charge of 'the girls'. It looks like the same person each time, with heavy black-rimmed glasses and a huge wig. With the Clara Wards, it was Momma Ward, Clara's mother. It was her job to see that all the younger singers were put to bed safely. If a concert finished at, say, 10.30 p.m., they all had to be in their rooms by 11.15 p.m.

Back in the hotel, we'd see Momma Ward looking in on all her charges to say goodnight before retiring to her own room. Five minutes later their doors would open one by one and they'd emerge, fully dressed, ready to go out on the town and enjoy themselves.

Humphrey Lyttelton

Did you know that, when they went through Ernest Hemingway's belongings after his death, they found dozens of Lee Wiley recordings but no other vocal records?

Benny Green

Huddie Ledbetter, frequently known as Leadbelly, had a fairly murky past. I can think of several crimes he committed, including murder twice and influencing Lonnie Donegan.

George Melly

Jack Jones regularly visits the club when he is in London. I remember one evening when we had a cashier on the door who was not really *au fait* with that sort of guest. She told Jack he could come in free but his friend would have to pay. His friend was Tony Bennett.

Ronnie Scott

I heard an old record the other day of Mike Cotton singing 'Heartaches' when he had his own band.

He plays trumpet with me these days but he doesn't do any singing. After hearing that record now I know why.

Acker Bilk

Here's a story about Billie Holiday which is not widely known. It involves jazz writer Max Jones who, as we all know, never missed a chance of interviewing and travelling around with visiting American jazz artistes.

► Billie Holiday pictured in London in April 1959, a month after the death of her long time platonic friend Lester Young who gave her the name 'Lady Day'. Within three months the greatest jazz singer of them all was dead herself after too many years of alcohol and drug abuse.

Billie Holiday had been doing a show in York and she allowed Max to convince her that it would be quicker and more comfortable to return to London in his car rather than travel by train like everyone else – and this was before motorways. Anyway, they got about an hour on the journey when Max's radiator sprang a leak. The road was absolutely deserted at the time, so Max had to replenish the radiator the best way he could. From then on his wife had to keep him topped up with bottles of beer so that he could keep stopping to rush round to the front of the car and refill the radiator.

Humphrey Lyttelton

I spent three of the most miserable weeks of my life 'minding' the old American Blues singer Jesse Fuller. He was a miserable sod, he did nothing but moan from morning till night.

You know he was a one-man band with things hanging around his neck and this amazing contraption he played with his big toe which he called a fotdella. I asked him where he got the name from and he told me his wife's name was Della and he played it with his foot.

George Webb

I remember when the Concord Club used premises at the Bassett Hotel in Southampton long before it moved to these sumptuous surroundings.

Back in those days there was an occasion when the Blues singer and pianist Champion Jack Dupree was booked as a guest with one of the bands. Well, when the club was still relatively empty by the intermission, the boss Cole Mathieson was getting really worried, especially as Champion Jack hadn't even turned up. Luckily, somebody came into the club and said, 'Here, you want to come to the public bar, there's an old black guy playing piano in there. It's absolutely packed out and the music is great.' Champion Jack Dupree had walked into the first bar, seen a piano and started playing.

John Barnes

We made an album with Lillian Boutté, currently the official 'Ambassador of Jazz' for New Orleans. Before the session, I sent her a cassette with versions of six songs which I thought we might record. I expected her to pick two or three, but she learnt all of them and they were on the record. The only problem was one track, 'Blue Again', in which she got a word wrong. In the verse, there's a line 'Love can do an awful lot of stunts'. Lillian misheard the cassette and sang 'Love can do an awful lot of stuff'. I didn't spot this until I was doing the final mixing, by which time Lillian was on tour in Germany.

The recording was done at Ted Taylor's studio down in Kent, so we got Ted's wife Lily, a singer herself, into the studio to record the syllable 'nts'. On the record, Lillian sings 'stu' and Lily sings 'nts'.

Humphrey Lyttelton

That was the most unlikely combination of Mae West singing with Duke Ellington's Orchestra in 1934 ['My Old Flame']. I think she was one of the great heroines of the twentieth century. Once she was up on a morals rap for presenting a dirty play and she was given ten days in jail. She got two days off for good behaviour, was allowed to wear silk underclothes while she was inside, and went out to dinner every night with the warden.

Benny Green

When Louis Jordan toured with my band in 1962, we actually got a phone call asking if he would do a *Sunday Night at the London Palladium*. Of course, they had mixed him up with the heart-throb film star Louis Jourdan.

I would have accepted if we hadn't already got a good booking. Can you imagine their faces if we had turned up?

Chris Barber

On our tour, Big Joe Turner asked me to help him buy a simple camera. On the way into Manchester we stopped at a camera shop and I asked the assistant for the simplest camera he had. He got out an Instamatic and was describing how all you had to do was load it, put it up to your eye and shoot, when Joe headed for the door.

Outside, I asked, 'What's the matter, Joe?' He said, 'Man, you've gotta go to school to work one of those.'

Humphrey Lyttelton

I like the story of the singing group Sweet Substitute arriving in Nottingham to play a new venue which they did not know. They pulled the bandwagon up beside a young policeman to ask for directions. After a puzzled pause, the policeman confessed he had no idea where the venue was, so the driver moved on. As they pulled away the drummer leant out of the window and shouted, 'No wonder you guys could never find Robin Hood.'

Roger Horton

When Betty Carter was singing at the club her trio was led by John Hicks on piano.

One night I was introducing the act and I was explaining that, before Betty came on, her wonderful trio would do a number on their own. Well, I remembered the drummer and bass player okay, but John Hicks's name had gone right out of my head, so I tapped the microphone, pretended it had gone off, excused myself, dashed over to the sound control booth and asked the sound man the name of the pianist and rushed back to the microphone, saying, 'Ah, the mike is working again, ladies and gentlemen – and John Hicks on piano.'

Ronnie Scott

Norma Winston is a presenter's nightmare. I'm always afraid I'm going to call her Norman Wisdom.

Even worse are Herman Autrey and Gene Cedric from the old Fats Waller band. Eventually, I did it on my radio programme. I actually announced, 'That was Gene Autrey on trumpet'!

Humphrey Lyttelton

BANDLEADERS

Bandleaders vary a great deal in style – from Duke Ellington, whose compositions, arrangements and presence created a Duke Ellington performance, to Bill McKinney, who was purely the manager of his Cotton Pickers. On the other hand, Jack Teagarden was a superb musician who was not a success as a leader, whereas Bob Crosby and Cab Calloway were singers who enjoyed immense success with their bands.

There is no doubt that some bandleaders developed into martinets and some even blatantly exploited their sidemen financially. I know of one British bandleader who allowed his band to live for a month in a caravan by an autobahn, melting snow for water while he stayed in a top Düsseldorf hotel.

Ted Lewis perpetrated one of the greatest frauds of all time on a record. When Benny Goodman was making a record with his band he arranged for all the musicians to shout out 'Play it, Ted' while Goodman was in the middle of a marvellous solo.

Benny Green

Ken Colyer was guesting with a local band and during the interval the bandleader was standing at the bar eating a bag of crisps when Ken came over to get a drink. So the bandleader turned to Ken remarking how well he thought the session was going, and Ken turned on him, saying, 'You're talking about music born out of anguish and all you can think about is food.'

Acker Bilk

Acker and I were standing at the bar in the 100 Club about five years ago having a drink when this beautiful young girl came up behind him and put her arms around his neck. Now I know Acker's missus, Ginger; I've known her for years. So I thought to myself, what's the old bugger been up to now? Then this lovely young thing said, 'Dad, have you got a cigarette?' Of course, it was his daughter Jenny, whom I hadn't seen since she was about a foot long.

Diz Disley

In my early days I worked in the Ambrose Orchestra. Ambrose had always been an idol of mine because he had such a fine band before the war; they were always on the radio and he must have made a lot of money.

Anyway, one night a 'Hooray Henry' sent up a request wrapped in a £1 note. Bert Ambrose looked at it, shook his head and sent it back wrapped in a £5 note.

Ronnie Scott

Here's a quote from the *Brighton Argus* dated February 1988: 'Celebrating 40 years as a Bandleader – Humphrey Lyttelton and his Band – a special THREAT for all jazz fans'.

Humphrey Lyttelton

I'd like to tell a funny story about Artie Shaw, but there aren't any.

Al Cohn

I heard a story about Artie Shaw putting yet another band together in 1951. They were playing a real hick town called Palacios on the Texas Gulf. It really was off the track and the clientele was comprised mainly of cowboys carrying bottles wrapped in brown paper because of the local licensing laws.

Anyway, as the evening went on Artie Shaw became aware

► Artie Shaw, Benny Goodman's rival who changed bands as often as wives: Lana Turner and Ava Gardner were amongst his changes of personnel.

of a little bloke who, every time he danced by the stage, kept winking at Shaw, suggesting he knew something special. Eventually Artie Shaw stopped this guy and asked him what all the winking was about. The little guy said he wouldn't tell anybody that he wasn't really Artie Shaw. So Shaw said, 'Supposing I tell you I am Artie Shaw?' The little guy laughed and said, 'Yeah, what would Artie Shaw be doing in a town like Palacios?'

Campbell Burnap

I found a lovely quote in a P. G. Wodehouse novel where a girl says to her mother, 'You know, when a girl goes to Hollywood she doesn't have to marry Artie Shaw; it is optional.'

Benny Green

Once, in the late Fifties, I was with Duke Ellington in his hotel suite when some London University students were interviewing him for their magazine. One of the more erudite among them asked Duke if he was offended when tenor sax player Jimmy Forrest borrowed a theme from his 'Happy-Go-Lucky Local' and had a huge hit with it under the title 'Night Train'.

Urbane as always, Duke said, 'No. It must be a good tune for so many people to want to write it.'

Humphrey Lyttelton

I worked for Charlie Barnet on several occasions. One time his manager Charlie Weintropp asked me to go to Hawaii with the band. I was only about twenty years old at the time so I was not really experienced at negotiating, but I knew enough to ask how much the job was worth. When I asked Charlie Weintropp about the money, he told me not to worry about money – 'We'll make you happy.' I told Charlie that wasn't good enough and that I wanted to know exactly how much money I would receive because we all have a different concept of happiness.

Actually, the Charlie Barnet Orchestra was one of the most ill-disciplined bands I have ever worked in, but it always sounded good because everybody had such a good time. Another thing, many people thought he had a large private income because his mother was a major stockholder in the New York Central Railroad, but she gave him very little support because she was disgusted that he was in the music business.

Barney Kessel

► Bandleader/saxophonist Charlie Barnet was born into a wealthy family and was a maverick amongst white bandleaders. He was a total fan of Duke Ellington, never hesitated in employing black musicians and had an all-out jazz policy. His 11 marriages put even Artie Shaw to shame.

I always think of Charlie Barnet as a real gentleman. For instance, on one occasion he hired the complete Duke Ellington Band to play for him at his birthday party and put a large sign on the front of the stage which read 'NO REQUESTS'.

Benny Green

Yes, it's perfectly true that Jimmy and Tommy Dorsey were always fighting. The real reason was that Jimmy had the better band until Tommy reorganised his band in 1940. I was in the band by then, and it helped that we had an unknown singer called Frank Sinatra.

Buddy Rich

Did you know that the comic Jimmy 'Schnozzle' Durante used to lead a jazz band? Only the other day I heard a record of 'Ja-Da' which he made way back in 1918 with his Original New Orleans Jazzband.

Humphrey Lyttelton

There were two leaders in that band. Vic Lewis on guitar, who is now a very successful theatrical agent, and Jack Parnell, who isn't.

Ronnie Scott

One of the things which endeared me to Alex Welsh, whose band must have played here in the 100 more than any other band – I should say a minimum of 250 appearances over a period of twenty years or more – was that never once did he get here on time. He could start on time at a concert in Glasgow but he could never get from the Cromwell Road to here in time to start at 8.30 p.m.

Roger Horton

Russell Quaye was an artist who led a skiffle group called the City Ramblers back in the late 1950s. His painting was, how can you say, in the style of the Aborigines as seen on the walls of caves in Australia – very much the same approach as his guitar playing.

Anyway, the first time I met Russell Quaye and his wife Hilda was at the Ballads and Blues Club in Holborn. They were a charming couple, in fact they asked me back to a party that very night. When I got to this party it was packed out with people playing kazoos and washboards and generally having a good time. Despite the place being full I did manage to spot a seat in the corner which was free, so I quickly grabbed it. I hadn't been there very long when I felt a peculiar sensation as if it was raining. It turned out that Russell Quaye had a pet monkey in a cage high up on the wall and that was why the seat was empty. Everybody knew about this except me.

Diz Disley

One of my earliest jobs back in the 1950s was with the Cy Laurie Band. Even then Cy was a vegetarian, which was almost unheard of in those days. Cy actually tried to convert everybody in the band to vegetarianism. He would take a couple of us at a time to his farm in Essex and subject us to a strict regimen which included no alcohol.

If I tell you that Diz Disley was on banjo at the time, you will not be surprised to learn that he disgraced himself by being found in the local pub with a foaming pint in one hand and a greasy pork pie in the other.

Alan Elsdon

Everybody knows about Benny Goodman's careful approach to spending money. A small example is that he would frequently visit the club with a couple of friends, eat dinner, drink a bottle of wine etc., and there was never any question of him paying. He would just stand up and walk out. So bearing that in mind I fully appreciated the story Bill Crow tells of Victor [Feldman] during the infamous tour of Russia they both did with Goodman.

Victor had a ciné camera with him and he managed to film Benny Goodman giving some small change to a starving child outside some monastery place. Since that day many musicians have enjoyed this film, which Victor runs backwards so it appears that Benny is taking the money from the kid.

Ronnie Scott

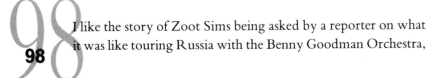

I like the story of Zoot Sims being asked by a reporter on what it was like touring Russia with the Benny Goodman Orchestra,

► Stan Getz and Benny Goodman – the meeting of the egos.

and Zoot replied, 'Every gig with Benny is like playing in Russia.'

Benny Green

Bobby Rosengarden was a witness to the well-worn story of the day Benny Goodman called a sextet rehearsal at his apartment and the guys complained of being cold. Benny immediately agreed, went out and returned wearing a thick pullover.

Dave Shepherd

I toured Italy with Benny Goodman in 1970. He asked me to play a trumpet feature, so I did my arrangement of 'I Can't Get Started'.

Every night he brought it in too fast, so one night when he announced it I shouted across to him, 'Can we have the right tempo tonight, Benny?' No. He brought it in as fast as usual, so I thought, sod him, I'll play it at my tempo. It was absolute chaos to start with, but as soon as the band 'found' me it was perfect.

Kenny Baker

I think Benny Goodman sometimes gets more criticism than he deserves from fellow musicians, because I can tell you of at least one occasion when the joke was on him and he laughed. It was at the time when Vido Musso was in the band.

Benny was never satisfied with his own clarinet reeds and he always found a way of 'borrowing' one from somebody else in the band. Vido Musso was the main provider at this time and, in order to get his own back, he started systematically every night to swap a part of his clarinet with Benny's, because they played the same model Selmer.

First night he switched the bell, then the lower joint, next night the upper joint and finally the barrel. So by now Benny is playing Vido Musso's clarinet as well as his reed. When Vido told him, Benny just broke up and laughed. However, I must say if it had been anybody else, they would have got an immediate 'ray' and instant dismissal. [Benny Goodman's disapproving glare was universally known as a 'ray'.]

Bob Wilber

I remember doing a gig at Southampton when I was with the George Webb Band around 1947. We had the jazz critic and writer Max Jones with us on the trip. Max is a diffident man, with a tendency to worry.

George, in common with many small men, has an abrupt, no-nonsense manner. When we got to the hall, a bit late, we didn't know how to get in. Max asked anxiously, 'Where's the front?' In his most assertive Cockney, George said, 'Round the back.'

Humphrey Lyttelton

Veteran pianist and bandleader George Webb was sitting at home one day having dinner. After the main course he looked at his wife Mina and complained that there was something important missing. Anyway, he got really upset because she'd forgotten that it was Shrove Tuesday and he had missed his beloved pancakes. That evening they hardly spoke to each other.

Next day, after he'd eaten his meal, Mina produced this covered dish. When he took off the lid he saw a load of burnt remains. 'Don't tell me you've forgotten that it's Ash Wednesday,' she said.

Alan Elsdon

I suppose my first professional job in the 'big time' was with Carlo Krahmer, even though I was only sixteen years old and I'd told Carlo I couldn't really play. Carlo said it didn't matter, but his tenor sax player had left the band and Jimmy Skidmore couldn't join for two weeks. He went on to say I didn't have to play anything as long as I looked convincing and he could fulfil his contract of producing seven musicians on stage. So I had two weeks' work just holding a saxophone in my mouth.

Ronnie Scott

I know Carlo Krahmer and his wife very well. I'll never forget the night I was sitting in their kitchen having a cup of tea with Greta Krahmer when we heard a noise coming from the bedroom. This was during the war when I was a sergeant in the army – don't laugh. Being a fully trained fighting man I decided I should investigate. As I pushed on the door I could feel it being resisted from the other side, so I pushed even harder and got the door open just wide enough to see the biggest burglar in the world – about 6 foot 6 inches tall.

You know you sometimes imagine what you would say if you found a dangerous intruder in your house. I'd always thought I would charm him by saying things like 'I hate the police', or, 'My uncle was a burglar', or even, 'I wish I was a burglar myself.'

As it turned out, I just winked at him, closed the door and locked it.

Alan Clare

My band toured alongside Eddie Condon's when they came over after the Musicians' Union ban had been lifted in the late 1950s.

One day we stopped at a little pub in the West Country for lunch. Having had a double Scotch for his 'breakfast', Eddie pushed his hat on the back of his head, strolled over to some local rustics, stared and then asked, 'Are you guys poachers?'

Humphrey Lyttelton

I well remember a 'live' recording with the Mulligan Band at the Railway Arms, West Hampstead.

There was a certain lady in the invited audience who thought she was in love with Mick. During a break she somehow managed to barricade herself in a side room with him. Not for long, I may add, because her husband tracked her down and kicked the door in. She turned on him furiously, saying, 'That's typical, you bloody well spoil everything, don't you?'

George Melly

You know neither Harry nor Laurie Gold are very tall. In fact there was a time when nobody in the Pieces of Eight was more than about 4 foot 6 inches tall.

The late Denis Preston told me about a time the Harry Gold Band was booked for a recording session at Bush House for the BBC Overseas Service. The control box at Bush House was unusually high up above the studio and Denis and Robin Scott were sitting in there drinking coffee while they waited for the band to turn up. After several cups of coffee, Denis remarked that he couldn't understand why the band had not arrived as they were usually so reliable.

Anyway, eventually one of them stood up, looked down into the studio and there was the band, all set up and waiting to play. They'd been there all along, out of sight below the control-room window.

Humphrey Lyttelton

In my early days I had some lessons from Harry Gold. He was very helpful, but the best tip he gave me was never to wear brown shoes with a blue suit.

Ronnie Scott

Ken Colyer was an enigma. We all know he liked a drink or four, but he was very strict with his bands about timekeeping.

One day on a tour the band was waiting in the foyer of an hotel when it was noticed that Ken was five minutes late for the bandcall; this was unheard of. At that moment the telephone on the reception desk rang and the receptionist asked for one of the band to go to Mr Colyer's room. So Graham Stewart, the trombonist, went off to see what the trouble was. When he got to Ken's room he found that Ken had lost his comb, and he refused to come out without combing his hair. Unfortunately, Graham was almost bald.

Monty Sunshine

I worked for the American bandleader Roy Fox, who claimed to have depped for Bix Beiderbecke in the Paul Whiteman Orchestra. I found him a very nice man except we parted under slightly strained circumstances.

We were working in Scotland around 1952 and I had recently fallen in love with someone who was not in Scotland. I asked to leave the band but Roy Fox refused to let me go. Later that evening he paid us all a lot of back money, and as it amounted to within £3 of what he owed me I thought this is as close as it's going to get, so I arranged a dep and quietly disappeared back to London. We didn't meet again for nearly twenty years, and when we did we decided to forget about the incident – he didn't ball me out and I didn't ask for my three quid.

Benny Green

Way back in the early 1950s my band shared the bill with the Sid Phillips Band. In those pre-motorway days we travelled to distant jobs by train.

The next day we were standing on the station platform when

▶ The charismatic drummer/bandleader Buddy Rich who was famous for his scathing opinions of mass appeal music.

a man came up to us, and it was obvious that he assumed we were in the Sid Phillips Band and furthermore that he was a long-standing fan of Sid Phillips, because he raved on about Sid with the Ambrose Band before the war, etc., etc. He went on to say what a kind man Sid appeared to be and then asked us what it was like working for such a wonderful man.

The temptation was too much for us. We told the man that Sid was an absolute monster to work with and gave lurid details. We left him looking disillusioned.

Humphrey Lyttelton

I frequently work with Keith Nichols, generally in his Fats Waller Band. On one occasion we were lined up for a promotional job which stipulated the band must wear straw hats. So Keith borrowed six very expensive straw hats from Laurie Chescoe, the drummer. These hats were from a famous West End hatter and must have cost at least £20 each. What Keith didn't realise was that these hats were put together with a special glue. But his dogs found out – they ate the lot.

Alan Elsdon

I never knew until after he had died that my father played cello when he was at Cambridge University.

I was going through his personal effects when I came across a profile of him in the university magazine. It read: 'When George Lyttelton practices the cello, all the cats in the district converge upon his rooms in the belief that one of their number is in distress.'

Humphrey Lyttelton

I worked for Stan Kenton and I must say he had one very sympathetic idea. He had two band coaches. One for the 'marrieds' and one for the 'singles', whose language, he maintained, was too strong for the wives.

Benny Green

For years, Louis Armstrong carried a personal valet, Doc Pugh, around with him. After years of faithful service, Doc died suddenly.

In Germany, one of the regular fans noticed his absence and Louis told him that Doc had died. Shocked, the fan asked, 'But vot is wrong viz him?' Louis said, 'When you're dead, pretty well everything's wrong with you.'

Humphrey Lyttelton

Pete Appleby was a most considerate drummer: his feature number was such a lengthy affair that we used to have time to slip out to the nearest hostelry for a drink.

After a while Mick [Mulligan] would go to the door, cock an ear towards the hall where we were playing, and say, 'Thank God, inspiration has descended; plenty of time for another drink.'

Actually, Mick doesn't play trumpet any more, but he is happy and free of fleas in Sussex, where he runs a garage. Also, as bad language has become a norm rather than the exception, he's allowed into several local pubs.

George Melly

Graeme Bell and his family stayed with me when he brought his band over from Australia in 1951 on their second tour here. I used to say that I had Australians like other people have mice. They kept turning up at Graeme's invitation. I'd meet a perfect stranger on the stairs and ask if he was looking for Graeme. He'd say, 'No . . . I live here.'

Humphrey Lyttelton

CHAPTER 8

THE BRITISH JAZZ SCENE POST-1960

This period starts with an explosion of jazz interest because it coincides with the Trad boom which made the three B's (Barber, Ball and Bilk) household names. Also the lifting of the Musicians' Union ban on American musicians meant that jazz fans could now see regular concerts by the likes of Count Basie, Duke Ellington and Woody Herman, as well as small groups and solo artistes in the 100 Club and the newly opened Ronnie Scott's.

Over the years this has provided our home-grown musicians with the priceless experience of backing world-class guests and the likes of Stan Tracey, Roy Williams, Ian Carr and John Barnes are just a few of the British musicians who have themselves acquired international reputations.

Jazz fans have also had a field day as they have been able to rub shoulders with their heroes such as Henry Red Allen or Wild Bill Davison at the bar during an intermission at the 100 Club. Or can you imagine the excitement of being in the Ronnie Scott Club to see Art Blakey's Jazz Messengers and wondering who the dazzling 19 year old kid on trumpet was and hearing the name Wynton Marsalis for the first time?

When Benny Goodman was over here touring with a specially formed band of British musicians he was fascinated by Bob Burns, who, as we all know, enjoys a sherry or two before lunch. Eventually, Benny asked him how he could play so well after drinking so much. 'It's easy,' Bob told him, 'I'm like this when I practise.'

John Barnes

We made that album in this very club [Ronnie Scott's]. I remember there was a lot of drink flowing about, which resulted in a couple of tracks having to be re-taken in the studio.

My main recollection, however, was the reckless abandon of the invited audience. At least one young lady went topless – not on that track, I may add, as you can tell from John Chilton's vibrato, which was still under control.

George Melly

I knew Jimmy Deuchar very well and it must be admitted he liked a drink. Now, Jimmy always slept in the nude and one time, when we were staying in an hotel after he'd had rather a lot to drink, he got up in the middle of the night to answer a call of nature. This involved poor Jimmy stumbling along the corridor naked looking for a bathroom.

Unfortunately his bedroom door slammed shut and he spent the next three hours hiding until the chambermaids came around.

Ronnie Scott

John Picard played trombone with my band for nearly ten years. At first he played a sort of rugged Dixieland style. Later he passed through mainstream jazz on to the avant garde, a fact which I discovered to my cost recently.

Promoters are always asking me to 'recreate' my earlier bands and we did one concert in Weston-super-Mare in which I had John Picard, Wally Fawkes and Kathy Stobart as guests, to represent my bands from the 1950s and 1960s.

At Sunday concerts in Weston-super-Mare the front three

rows are taken up by elderly ladies of frail disposition. When John came on for his set, he immediately switched into his avant-garde mode. When it came to his first solo he got so close to the microphone that it was actually inside the bell of the trombone, and unleashed a stentorian bellow which must have shunted most of the front row straight into intensive care.

Humphrey Lyttelton

I remember back in the 1960s, when I was with the Alex Welsh Band, we were playing a gig at the Shakespeare Theatre Club in Liverpool. Roy Williams had spotted two very attractive girls in the front of the audience, so it was with added enthusiasm that he went into his solo feature on 'Tangerine'. This involved playing a few trombone choruses and then singing, after which he smiled at the girls and nonchalantly swaggered to the side of the stage while the pianist had a solo chorus.

As he walked along he emptied his spit valve, and one of these girls turned to the other and said, 'Ooh, the dirty bugger.'

John Barnes

I knew a pianist who used to play a lot of solo work in classy restaurants, where he had to endure being incessantly interrupted in the middle of a number by 'Hoorays' asking him to play their favourite tunes. He got so fed up with this he had some cards printed which he kept on top of the piano so he could pass them out. On the card it said, 'Sod off, I'm working.'

Actually, Alan Clare used to do a lot of this work, and one day a 'Hooray' approached him and asked for 'You Are the One'. Alan said he didn't know the song, could he sing it. 'Certainly,' said the 'Hooray', 'Night and day, you are the one.'

Ronnie Scott

Kenny Clare always played marvellous and inventive drum solos with my big band. I remember playing a firemen's dance in Hull one night when Kenny really excelled himself. One of these firemen came up to me, saying that Kenny's drumming was absolutely fantastic. 'But, mind you, we've got a bloke who plays in a pub around the corner who's even better.'

John Dankworth

I love the story which Jack Parnell tells about Irish jazz guitarist Louis Stewart. Stewart got booked to play with an avant-garde group and complained afterwards they sounded like a pet shop on fire.

Kenny Baker

I always remember with great affection the banjo player Stu Morrison, but unfortunately, after yet another misdemeanour, he got the bullet from the Chris Barber Band. Anyway, he soon got the job with the Ken Colyer Band, but as Ken wasn't working all that much at the time Stu got a day job as a gardener at Regent's Park.

By sheer chance this all happened with my moving house and trying to establish a herbaceous border in my back garden. For some months, every time the Colyer Band played here at the 100, Stu arrived with boxes of azaleas and delphiniums, saying these were 'surplus to requirements at Regent's Park'.

Roger Horton

I saw an advertisement in *The Times* for a concert in the Purcell Room which read 'The Eddie Johnson Trio with Roy Thompson on Trimbine'.

It should have read 'The Eddie Thompson Trio with Roy Williams on Trombone'.

Digby Fairweather

When I used to run a sextet with Al Gay, we were once billed as the 'All Gay Joan Barnes Sextet'.

Another time, at a Portman Hotel gig I was playing with Roy Williams, we were billed as the 'Jolly Barnes Quartet plus Boy Williams'.

John Barnes

There's a story about Phil Seamen when he was playing drums with the pit orchestra for *West Side Story*, which has a very tricky score with lots of time changes; Phil could handle all that sort of thing. Incidentally, Al Cohn has a very simple theory about how to play in 5/4 time. You just play in 4/4 and add a bar.

Anyway, back to Phil and *West Side Story*. One night he nodded off to sleep during a quiet spot and fell off his stool and up against a big gong. With great presence of mind, he stood up and announced, 'Dinner is served.'

Ronnie Scott

I actually started out by playing clarinet. Back in 1963 I joined a band in Southend-on-Sea which already had an excellent trumpet player – John Shillito. Not only was he a good trumpet player, but he also performed a marvellous one-man cabaret on the sea front which involved a Venus de Milo with a movable jaw and a bass drum which lit up to say 'BANG'.

Digby Fairweather

I remember one of my first efforts at going out as a solo act making guest appearances with local bands and rhythm sections. This job was in Huddersfield, and at the end a bluff Yorkshireman came up to me enquiring if I was the trombone player. When I confirmed that I was, he said, 'Yes, I like the trombone, no matter how it is played.'

Campbell Burnap

Running a club with the sort of eclectic policy we have, which covers most styles of jazz, blues and fusion, I get some strange callers at my office.

One afternoon there was a knock on the door and there stood a huge black fellow with a massive Afro hair style. Before he could say a word I told him that I was totally booked out for months ahead and I couldn't handle any more bands. 'That's very interesting', he said. 'I'm from the Inland Revenue.'

Roger Horton

When the Stones' drummer Charlie Watts appeared in the club with his big band, it really was a big band; it was enormous. Apart from Charlie there were two other drummers, seven or eight saxophone players, and so on (right down to two vibes players). I think there were thirty-five of them altogether.

I remember listening to them rehearse one afternoon as I was passing through the club. At the end of one opus one of the drummers enquired if the tempo was okay. To which a voice from the sax section said, 'Great. I liked all three tempos.'

Ronnie Scott

I play clarinet once or twice a night. I've actually got a rarity – an export reject student's instrument made of plastic. When I told Kenny Davern he said, 'Don't worry, I play one made of hard compressed rubber.' And he wasn't joking. Apparently it's the latest invention.

Humphrey Lyttelton

I remember when I was playing with the Alex Welsh Band in Barnsley, a chap came up to me in the interval and remarked that I hadn't played much clarinet, but rather more alto and baritone saxes. He went on to ask if I had ever considered dropping the clarinet altogether and becoming 'fully modernised'.

John Barnes

Trombonist John Mortimer and drummer Johnny Richardson used to work together in a band and, like all touring musicians, they used to get upset with the cleaning ladies in hotels who start hoovering outside your bedroom door at 9.00 am if you haven't got up for breakfast.

Anyway, Messrs Mortimer and Richardson developed this ploy of finding the cupboard which housed the vacuum cleaners as soon as they booked into a hotel and cut the plugs off.

Digby Fairweather

That was the late and very much missed Herr Lennie Hastings, who had this peculiar empathy with the German nation. At the drop of a hat he would insert a monocle in his eye and sing those hilarious songs in fractured German. Incidentally, he was an excellent drummer as well as being so funny.

One of his favourite tricks at the end of a session was to whip off his wig. He had very unlikely wigs; only Earl Hines had wigs which were less like human hair. Anyway, he would snatch his wig off and throw it high in the air while he played rapid rimshots with his left hand. Meanwhile the stick in the right hand would pretend to shoot at it as it descended, and he'd announce to the audience, 'Ladies and gentlemen, the grouse season is open.'

George Melly

I remember seeing Lennie Hastings having an argument outside the Blue Posts, the pub behind the 100 Club. A few yards away was a policeman with a dog. I think he was a jazz fan because he was quite happily engrossed in conversation with some of the Alex Welsh musicians. Anyway, this policeman hadn't realised that his dog had walked around him a couple of times wrapping its lead around his ankles.

Meanwhile, Lennie was getting really steamed up and he snatched off his wig and threw it on the ground. The dog dived at the wig and the policeman did a somersault.

Jack Fallon

I was driving the Alex Welsh bandwagon to Manchester one day when we got stopped by the police just as we left the motorway. This copper stuck his head through the open window and went, 'Oo-ya, oo-ya, what time are you on tonight?'

John Barnes

Vic Ash is the only clarinet player I know who has got one brown eye and one blue one – which is interesting as well as boring.

Ronnie Scott

▶ The greatest British jazz drummer Phil Seaman who died in his mid-40s in 1972. Seen here with Stan Tracey and Stan Wasser (*bass*).

I made an LP with the Stan Tracey Big Band. It was called 'Blue Acker' and they had me pictured on the cover sitting on this huge block of ice. I got so paralysed during the photo session that they had to find me a piece of wood to sit on.

Acker Bilk

I saw the stage show *One Mo' Time* on several occasions. It was most enjoyable.

The storyline was about the various artistes who had worked on the TOBA, which was generally known as 'Tough on Black Arses'. It was the agency circuit for black performers in the southern States.

George Webb

Many years ago the banjo player Hugh Rainey worked for me. The band went off early one morning to fly to Paris, and as Hugh's wife and my wife were catching a later flight I left two tickets for them at an airline desk at Heathrow Airport.

Naturally, they arrived late, just in time to hear a public address announcement saying, 'Would Mrs Sunshine and Mrs Rainey please report to collect their flight tickets.'

Monty Sunshine

I remember when I was in Monty Sunshine's band and we stopped at an isolated pub way out in the country for a lunch-time drink. The pub was empty apart from an old guy washing some glasses and his mangy dog slumped on the floor.

Soon after we had got our order and settled down, a couple of 'county' ladies came in and enquired in rather superior voices if there was any food available. The publican offered them either ham or cheese sandwiches, and they settled for ham.

When their sandwiches arrived the dog suddenly came to life. He plonked himself next to them and sat staring at the plate. One of these women turned to the publican and said, 'I say, is your dog so hungry?'

'No,' replied the publican, 'I expect he's just a bit worried because you're using his plate.'

Campbell Burnap

Bireli Lagrene worked at the club three or four years ago with his quartet. They were all gypsies who looked like gangsters from a 1940s French movie – you only needed Jean Gabin for the complete set.

Actually, they were all country boys and at that time there was a striperama peep-show across from us in Frith Street. Every interval they went over there and I had to send somebody out to get them back on stage.

Ronnie Scott

Tenor-sax player Jimmy Skidmore was in my band for a long time. He's the sort of person who would have been described as a 'card' in Edwardian times. He calls everyone 'darling' – including a New York cop when we were over there in 1959.

▶ Tenor sax player Jimmy Skidmore – practical joker and father of Alan.

The guy bawled him out for jay-walking and he said, 'Sorry, darling!' There was almost a nasty scene.

Outrageous is the word for Jim. I'll never forget the night, some years after he left my band, when we were booked together at the Plough, Stockwell. He'd recently had all his bottom teeth out and was running in new dentures. I was playing what I thought was an exquisite solo, and it was moving towards its very emotional and moving climax when the audience started roaring with laughter. I kept going to the end of the solo, then turned and looked at Jim. He had his false teeth draped over his left ear.

Humphrey Lyttelton

I was playing with the Merseysippi Jazzband in the new Cavern Club in Liverpool. It is not the old cellar but a reconstruction; it looks like the old one, but clean. There are lots of murals and mementos but no mention that it used to be a jazz club long before the rot set in.

We played all the usual Merseysippi repertoire – 'Creole Belles', 'Come Back Sweet Papa' and that sort of thing. Towards the end of the evening a woman came up to the band to request 'Greensleeves'. Johnny Lawrence politely declined, saying that it was not in their repertoire, to which she retorted, 'Yes, I suppose it's very difficult for you down here as you have to play all that Beatles rubbish.'

John Barnes

A couple of years back I was in Liverpool for the celebration of the fortieth anniversary of the Merseysippi Jazzband.

As I was standing at the bar listening to the band and having a drink with Mick Mulligan, I spotted Frank Parr, who played trombone with the Merseysippi before he came to London to join Mick. Frank looked particularly sober and I commented to Mick that Frank was pacing himself really well. Mick agreed with me, but went on to say that in the old days they used to stick a supermarket label on him which said 'Best before 8.30 pm.'

Campbell Burnap

I played for about a year with the Rod Mason Band in the late 1970s. I remember the night I joined the band because they picked me up about 3.00 am *en route* for a continental tour. I climbed into the bandwagon, which roared off only to pull up sharply at the end of my road, and a laughing maniac rolled out of a bunk and dropped into my lap. He was the drummer – James Miles Garforth.

Jimmy still laughs a lot, despite living in Zürich, where he is playing beautifully with the Piccadilly Six and cooks a damned fine curry.

Dick Charlesworth

Bass player Tony Bagot told me a story about Rod Mason which took place about 1970, when he led a band based in his home town of Plymouth. In those days Rod was renowned for enjoying a few drinks – not like the reformed character we see these days when he comes over from Germany and frightens the life out of us native trumpeters.

Anyway, the band had been playing a gig in Bodmin. Rod decided to stay on for an after-hours drink, so four of them went home in the banjo player's car and Tony was left to drive Rod home in the band bus, an old Bedford ambulance. When they eventually set off for Plymouth, Rod immediately went to sleep in the back and Tony was left to negotiate those winding Cornish lanes without any moral support. Needless to say, he missed one of the bends, hit a bank and the bus finished up on its roof. Poor old Tony was trapped behind the steering wheel, so he called out to Rod to help him. 'Shut up you silly sod, I'm trying to get some sleep,' came the reply.

Alan Elsdon

Art Themen works most of the time with Stan Tracey and is not only a very talented saxophone player but also a practising orthopaedic surgeon.

He told me once how that very afternoon he'd had a consultation with a woman dressed in rags who, when she undressed, was positively filthy. He told her he couldn't possibly examine her in that condition and that she should go home, have a bath and then come back. She then told him that she had already seen another consultant who had given her the same advice. So Art asked her why she had come to him and she told him she wanted a second opinion.

Ronnie Scott

Funnily enough, the bass player Don Smith, who is now a BBC photographer, is sitting in the audience at this very moment. Don took my wedding photographs. I am still waiting for them, and my silver wedding comes up next March.

John Barnes

▶ 'Shut up you silly sod, I'm trying to get some sleep came the reply.' The
Rod Mason Band pictured on Plymouth Hoe in Sept. 1969. *L to R:* Roy
Pellett, Peter Sumner, Sir Francis Drake, Jimmy Garforth, Rod Mason,
Tony Bagot and Bobbie Fox.

I made a record for the *Stomp Off* label with the French clarinet
player Jean-François Bonnel. When I first spoke to him he just
stared back at me like a startled gazelle, so from then on it was
pidgin-English and sign language.

It wasn't till we were packing up at the end that I heard him
talking to one of the other musicians in perfect English.

Humphrey Lyttelton

I love motor racing. I'll never forget my first race at Brands
Hatch; it was for BMW owners.

I was absolutely paralysed with fear and when the flag
dropped I slammed my foot down on the accelerator – but
nothing happened except everybody else disappeared out of
sight. It took me about five seconds to realise I'd still got the
handbrake on.

Ronnie Scott

Trumpet player Keith Smith lived in Cornwall for a time, where his house backed onto open farmland. When the mood took him he would stroll around the garden playing his trumpet and sometimes he even ventured into the adjoining field.

One day he noticed a Landrover approaching him. A farmer stepped out and the following conversation ensued:

' 'Ere, you've been bugling in my field.' – 'Yes.'

'It's not the first time is it?' – 'No.'

' 'Ere, what's my field like for bugling in?'

Digby Fairweather

Bobby Wellins is a great tenor sax player, but he did go through an awkward period at one time. In fact he's the only guy I know who has been banned from Ron Mathewson's flat.

Ronnie Scott

Two friends of mine, Freddy Clayton and Johnny McLevy, have got identical trumpet cases. They had been on a recording session together, finished the date and went their separate ways.

That evening Freddy phones Johnny to tell him that they must have picked up the wrong trumpet cases, and went on to say that he could manage the trumpet and the mouthpiece but he couldn't make the dentures fit.

Kenny Baker

Kenny Baker has recently completed the mammoth task of re-recording all of Louis Armstrong's classic recordings on CD. Everything is there from Hot Fives and Hot Sevens to big band numbers. I think it was financed with German money. They certainly had a German musical director because he turned to the running order one day and said, 'Gentlemen, I think we'll go through thirty-nine to forty-five again', and one of the band was heard to say, 'I never thought I'd hear a German say that.'

Campbell Burnap

I've got a soprano saxophone at home, but I wouldn't dare play it in public. I discussed this problem with Zoot [Sims] and he told me that he'd gone through this phase and in fact gave up playing it, until one day he was in a music store where he picked up a soprano and everything clicked.

Since then I try out all the sop saxes in every music shop I visit – it hasn't worked yet!

Ronnie Scott

My trombonist Micky Cooke told me of an occasion when he was with the Terry Lightfoot Band and they had to play some out-of-the-way spot in the West Country.

When they arrived the chaps in the band urged Terry to go in and find out if there was a house PA system, as they could get away earlier for the long drive to London if they didn't have to use the band's system.

Terry went in and found a bartender, who confirmed there was a built-in house PA system. When he asked what kind, the bartender assured him with great authority that it was 'electric'.

Acker Bilk

One night my band played a ballroom in Swindon. Towards the end of the evening my bass player, Mick Gilligan, tripped up and landed on top of his bass, which snapped in half.

Come the end of the night, we were packing up with just the band and a solitary figure sweeping up. As he swept past the band, he looked at the remains of the bass and muttered, 'I always wondered how you packed those things away.'

Alan Elsdon

Colin Smith went through a period of trying to research the meaning of all those strange titles which Louis Armstrong recorded in the 1920s – tunes like 'SOS Blues', 'Skip the Gutter', 'Static Strut' and 'Drop that Sack'. The one that stumped him was 'Yes, I'm in the Barrel'. He looked up *Webster's Dictionary of American Slang*; he tried everything, until one night he came into the Pizza Express, where he was playing with the All Stars, and as he was getting his trumpet out he announced he'd solved the puzzle. 'It was the answer to the question – are you in the barrel?'

Digby Fairweather

I tried teaching myself to play guitar at one time. I'd get home about 3.00 am and start playing my little D minor/A7th exercise; it was enough to send anybody crazy.

Well, one morning there was this almighty thumping on the floor above, because the guy upstairs couldn't take any more. When I got up later that morning, I found a note had been pushed through my letter-box from this neighbour, which went on about not understanding how a man of my intelligence could make this dreadful twanging noise in the middle of the night.

I know the chap to *nod* to, he's okay – in fact he's a lecturer of economics somewhere. So, I put a note through his door apologising for the disturbance but explained that I had Andrés Segovia staying in the spare bedroom.

Next morning back comes another note to say it was an honour and privilege to be woken up at 3.00 am by Señor Segovia and would I please pass on his best wishes to the maestro.

Ronnie Scott

That wonderful Scots character Stan Greig phoned me up and offered me a gig playing a tribute to Glenn Miller. I reminded Stan that I wasn't a very good reader so maybe he should book someone else, but he assured me it was only a five-piece busking job. When I queried how we could make a tribute to Glenn Miller with a quintet, he told me not to worry and that he'd got all that worked out.

So we turn up at this pub near Golders Green which is decked out in posters and pictures of Glenn Miller and absolutely jammed full with Miller fans. Stan's opening announcement was marvellous. He told the audience we were going to play 'Rosetta', and immediately there were a few raised eye-

► The Temperance Seven looking East in expectation as they were soon to make an album 10 miles up in the air at twice the speed of sound on the inaugural flight of Concorde in Bahrain – is this a record?

brows so he followed up by saying, ' "Rosetta" was Glenn Miller's mother's favourite tune.'

Campbell Burnap

The Temperance Seven recorded an album on the inaugural flight of Concorde to Bahrain sometime in 1976 [31 March]. That takes some beating, making a record ten miles up at twice the speed of sound.

However, my favourite story concerning the Temps is when they were booked to play at the Goose Fayre, which I think is in Nottingham. Anyway, the roadie arrived early with all their gear and he noticed that there was no piano on the open-air stage. He found the organiser, who assured him a grand had been ordered and everything would be okay by the evening.

Eventually the band arrived, but when there were no signs of the piano by 7.00 pm they began to worry, so one of them went off to the entrance and enquired if anybody had seen a piano arrive. 'Sure,' said a security man, 'we sent it straight down to the piano-smashing contest about two hours ago.'

Digby Fairweather

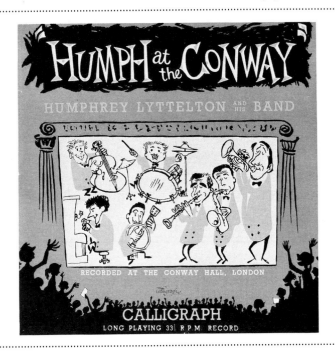

'Humph at the Conway' was an album I made back in 1954 and it has just been re-released (1986) as a reproduction album. By reproduction, I mean with the original cover design and sleeve note which refers to our playing a concert every month in the Conway Hall in London.

The funny thing is that about a week ago I received a letter from a young man saying that he had bought the record and this was just the sort of jazz concert he would like to visit, so could I tell him when the next one was. He went on to point out that he'd passed the Conway Hall recently and that I ought to know that there were no posters outside publicising our concerts.

Humphrey Lyttelton

8

MORE MUSICIANS'

HUMOUR

A further ration of this key ingredient in the success of *Jazz Score*. Incidentally, Ronnie Scott frequently uses the gag 'I'm not really a comedian but we do have one in the club – the chef.' I can assure you he definitely is the resident comedian on *Jazz Score*, and I make no apologies for quoting him so extensively.

There were so few people in the club to start with last Monday that we opened up with 'Tea for One'.

Ronnie Scott

I remember playing with Art Tatum when he played 'Tea for Two' with his left hand in B flat and his right hand in A flat. Later on he shifted both hands up half a tone.

Slim Gaillard

I played with a piano player like that last night.

Ronnie Scott

You know Ron Mathewson, the bass player, has a glass eye? Well, when Ron and I were in the Alex Welsh Band we used to get his spare glass eye, which he kept in an old matchbox, and put it on a table together with Jim Douglas's false teeth

125

and Lennie Hastings's wig. We used to make up this face and call him the eighth member of the band.

John Barnes

Of course, Ron Mathewson works with me now. I can always tell which is Ron's glass eye – it's the one with a glimmer of humanity in it.

Ronnie Scott

Sometimes British musicians' sense of humour is not always understood in Germany.

There is a story of when Ronnie Simmons was playing lead trumpet with Kurt Edelhagen's Band years ago. Apparently, during a recording session as they finished some big number Ronnie was screaming away on a top Z and just missed by a whisker as Kurt Edelhagen cut the band off. Edelhagen actually detected this and suggested they go for another take.

Had Ronnie been at home here he would have said 'Oh, Mrs Smith in Northampton won't notice that', but being in Germany he said in his best German 'Oh, Frau Schmidt in Hamburg won't notice that'. Kurt Edelhagen thought for a moment and then quite seriously said – 'Who is this Frau Schmidt?'

Eddie Harvey

Ron Rubin told me the story of being in the company of Tony Coe in an Indian restaurant in Hampstead recently. In the middle of their meal Tony spotted a rusty pin in his food. Without any fuss he quietly called the manager over, pointed out the offending article and said, 'For two pins I'd call the police.'

Campbell Burnap

The bass player Ron Rubin always used to refer to the Spanish dictator as 'Bloody de Franco'.

Ronnie Scott

That would be jazz cricketer Frank Parr. Did you know he was wicket keeper for Lancashire at one time? He also enjoys the occasional drink. In fact, he is known to his intimates as

'Catch a falling Parr'. Yes, a lovely man, a very fine trombonist with a great sense of humour.

George Melly

Talking about putting new tunes on top of old chords, I have just acquired an album of the National Youth Jazz Orchestra on which some bright young thing has taken the chords of 'Thou Swell' and turned it into a bebop extravaganza called 'Gynaecology'.

Digby Fairweather

Did you know that Chick Corea is a devout Scientologist? I know because he won't switch on the electric lights on Saturdays. He has to get a non-Scientologist to come in and do it for him.

Ronnie Scott

Al Cohn and Zoot Sims were great buddies of mine who both had a beautiful sense of humour. Al would say things like 'Let's play a game all the family can join in; it's called Incest.'

Another time Zoot told me that during World War Two all the American mothers would castigate their children for leaving food on their plates by saying, 'Come on, you've got to eat everything up because people in Europe are starving.'

Well, Zoot told me he was sitting in a bar one day when he saw a bloke with a strip of benzedrine from an inhaler. He tore the strip in half, put one half in his coffee and threw the other half away, to which Zoot commented, 'Come on man, people in Europe are sleeping.'

Ronnie Scott

Lester Young's brother, Lee, plays excellent drums. He's also good at golf; he cheats a lot, but he's pretty good.

Herb Ellis

A friend of mine set up some dates for the Great Guitars [Barney Kessel, Herb Ellis and Charlie Byrd] in Scotland and I got roped in as a sort of tour manager for a few days.

One day I arranged to take the guys to see the Queen's Scottish home at Balmoral. On the way our taxi got stuck behind a tractor and haycart on one of those little highland roads and we hardly moved for about ten minutes. All of a sudden, Barney Kessel turned to our elderly Scottish driver and confided, 'If I was on my way to the electric chair I'd want this guy in front to be the driver.'

Campbell Burnap

Do you remember the names we used to make up when we were on the road? There was the girl singer – Sheil O'Blige; the drunken Spanish guitarist – Segovia Yercarpet; the Australian pianist – Kenny Reid.

How about the German trumpet player – Mannheim Stoned; the scruffy Indian roadie – Ram Shackle; the French band-leader – Charles Louis d'Inse?

Benny Green and Ronnie Scott

Accompanying tap-dancers is like trying to play with someone bombarding you with Smarties.

Humphrey Lyttelton

That would be on the Miracle record label. Their motto was – 'If it's a good record, it's a miracle.'

Ronnie Scott

A folk singer is someone who sings through his nose by ear.

Diz Disley

A folk singer is someone who stays in bed all day and goes out in the evening and sings worksongs.

Benny Green

Wynton Marsalis has a brother named Branford who plays excellent tenor sax. He's known as Bran Marsalis, which makes him sound like a Greek breakfast.

Ronnie Scott

There's a story about Charlie Shavers being interviewed by the press in his London hotel room, when he pointed to the electric shaving point in the wall which was marked 'shavers only' and he said, 'Wait till Eldridge gets a look at that.'

Alan Elsdon

I was so impressed when I first heard Charlie Shavers that I bought the company.

Ronnie Scott
(with apologies to a certain TV commercial)

When I was touring Scandinavia with the Jack Parnell Orchestra back in the 1950s, I came across the bass player Chubby Jackson and his sextet. Apparently they were in a show with an amazing juggler and contortionist. Anyway, one night Chubby Jackson decided to play a joke on this contortionist by telling the audience that he was stone deaf, and therefore applause meant absolutely nothing to him. Instead, he told the audience that at the end of the man's act he wanted everybody to stand up and wave their handkerchiefs at him.

The poor bloke went through his amazing routine and finished standing on his finger, but when he took his bow all he could see was the audience waving goodbye in total silence.

They took him away in an ambulance.

Ronnie Scott

Tony Crombie leads a trio at the Kensington Hilton, and on one occasion around Easter time a 'Hooray' lady came up to the bandstand asking if they could play any Easter music. There was silence, then the pianist Bob Holloway looked up and grudgingly informed her 'I suppose we could play "East of the Sun".'

Alan Elsdon

Tony Crombie once told me of a restaurant where it was so clean you could almost eat off the plates.

Benny Green

Brian Lemon met Kenny Davern on the London Underground and told him he had an appointment with his accountant. Kenny remarked that was a coincidence as he had just heard from his accountant in the States, who told him he had just become a 'hundredaire'.

Roger Horton

Don Weller is a good tenor player with a lovely sense of humour. He told me that he went out with a girl the other night who was covered in bruises. When he asked her how she had got them, she told him it was other guys touching her with barge poles.

Ronnie Scott

The trombonist Bill Harris looked so respectable that you would think he was a doctor or a businessman, but actually he was a master practical joker.

For instance, he would eat out with friends in a very smart restaurant and when the meal was over he would put a pill in his mouth which immediately started foaming profusely. Other diners would look most concerned as this gibbering man foaming at the mouth was led from the restaurant complaining about the food.

Another thing he would do is enter the elevator in a tall building with a friend who would talk to him as if he was a doctor. You know how confined it is in an elevator and any conversation is completely audible. Well, this friend would turn to Bill Harris and say, 'Doctor, are you sure about performing that brain surgery this afternoon, because I know you've drunk at least four Martinis.'

Bill Harris would reply, 'Sure, I feel lucky today. In this business you win a few and lose a few.'

Barney Kessel

▶ The demure looking Bill Harris was in reality only rivalled by Joe Venuti for playing practical jokes. He was one of the great big band trombonists who could play with tremendous fire or delicate finesse.

Charlie Ventura led a quartet which he called his Big Four. The name always amused me because we used to call the big four sausage, egg, beans and chips.

Ronnie Scott

I like the story of the neurotic bandleader who was pacing up and down the pavement outside a club because his pianist was ten minutes late. All of a sudden the pianist pulls up on his motor bike. He's got nasty tyre marks across his crash helmet, blood pouring down the side of his face and the knee torn out of his trousers. Anyway, he apologises for being late and says it will only take him a couple of minutes to clean up and he will be on stage.

The bandleader just stood there looking up at the heavens and said, 'God. Why does everything have to happen to me?'

Acker Bilk

I remember Kirk Douglas played a Bix Beiderbecke-type character in the film *Young Man with a Horn*. In the book he dies before he can marry the girl, but in the film he has a fate worse than death – he lives long enough to marry Doris Day.

Benny Green

There was this guy who used to come regularly to the club. His name was Joe Burns; he was a cocktail pianist but he had a good sense of humour. His business card read:

> JOE BURNS, Pianist Entertainer
> 'Pissed or sober, a f----ing good act.'
> *(News Chronicle)*

Sometimes he would bring his wife with him and introduce her by saying, 'This is the wife – I'm sorry.'

Ronnie Scott

Trombonist Micky Cooke worked with me for many years and he is a very funny man. I remember him describing another British trombonist as the only guy who fills in a form for the Performing Wrong Society after each job.

Alan Elsdon

We had a group of gospel singers at the club once called the Stars of Faith. I remember the leader telling me that one of the girls had a drink problem, but she got it all sorted out when she joined Alcoholics Anonymous – now she drinks under a false name.

Ronnie Scott

▶ Al Cohn (*left*) and Zoot Sims played from 1947–50 in the bands of Woody Herman and Artie Shaw. Their swinging and inventive partnership continued off and on over the years including some very fine albums.

One night, after an exceptionally drunken trumpet solo, Mick Mulligan turned to Frank Parr and said, 'There you are, cock, all the volume and vulgarity of Freddy Randall with none of the technique.'

George Melly

Humphrey Lyttelton told me that Eddie Condon held a press reception in his London hotel room when he came over to Britain in 1957. Unfortunately, Condon was flat out, face down on the bed. Somebody asked him if he could sit up as his comments were not very clear. His reply was that he'd tried sitting up, but he was no athlete.

Acker Bilk

THE AMERICAN
JAZZ SCENE

This chapter deals with accounts of the American jazz scene either as told by American musicians who have appeared on *Jazz Score* or as anecdotes passed on to British musicians over the years.

Most of these stories relate to earlier times because it seems to me that around the 1960s the focus of jazz interest moved from the USA to Europe.

For a long time the best American jazz musicians were able to exist on studio work – making albums, film sound-tracks and playing in TV studio bands – but even the supremely accomplished drummer Bobby Rosengarden told me a few years ago that much of this work had also disappeared because of electronic substitutes. I understand that the most activity these days on the American and Canadian jazz scene is the very extensive network of jazz festivals, which has been mirrored by the explosion of festivals in Britain in recent years.

I used to play jam sessions on Sunday afternoons in a Hollywood club called The Capri with Teddy Bunn and his Spirits of Rhythm. All sorts of musicians like Lester and Lee Young would come by, also Billie [Holiday] would drop in, as well as film stars like Robert Taylor, Lana Turner, Gary Cooper, Barbara Stanwyck and all that crowd.

Norman Granz would always be there with his brother Oscar, who was too young to be a guest so he was kept

135

busy running across the street taking orders for hamburgers. Actually, Norman Granz was as broke as the Tenth Commandment, and he used to feed up for a week on those hamburgers. Also he worked out an arrangement with the Armed Forces Radio whereby he would tape the shows and sell them.

Years later I met Norman with Oscar Peterson and he introduced me as the man who used to feed him.

Slim Gaillard

One time in Hollywood I was asked by an agent to write four arrangements for a young singer he was grooming. He suggested I should phone this singer to arrange a meeting so that I could ascertain his vocal range and discuss the arrangements.

So I phoned this kid up and put the idea to him, but he assured me that it wasn't necessary to meet because he knew his vocal range. He told me he could sing up to one tone below the highest note in 'Who's Sorry Now'.

Barney Kessel

You know when Shelly Manne opened a club which he called Shelly's Manne-Hole, the trumpeter Manny Klein threatened to open a club called Manny's Klein-Hole?

Ronnie Scott

Roland Hanna worked with Benny Goodman in the late 1950s, but eventually they fell out over Hanna's piano playing for some reason. Anyway, there was a bit of a scene and Roland Hanna and Goodman did not part company on very friendly terms.

About twenty years later Roland gets a call to attend a rehearsal with Goodman. Apparently Benny looked at Roland and said, 'Aren't I supposed to hate you?'

Bob Wilber

While I was in New York in 1965 I visited Jimmy Ryan's and met the drummer Zutty Singleton, who turned out to be a very keen baseball fan. Furthermore, he told me that Art

► Tenor sax legend Coleman Hawkins with Jazz at the Phil boss Norman Granz whose JATP package shows began as a one-off concert in 1944.

Tatum, despite being virtually blind, was an absolute baseball fanatic. He could recall all the averages and figures and loved following the game with the aid of companions.

Of course, I often used to see Eddie Thompson at Lord's, and he was totally blind – he was a total cricket nut.

Campbell Burnap

Tipples were miniature guitars with ten strings – something like a mandolin. The brothers Wilbur and Douglas Daniels used to play them with the Spirits of Rhythm. Actually, they were very popular with singers and singing groups in the 1930s.

Slim Gaillard

There's an interesting story about the tune 'Slow Mood' which was written by tenor sax player Eddie Miller.

137

Some years after he'd written it he was playing a studio session at Capitol Records when Johnny Mercer poked his head around the door to say hello to everybody and Eddie called out reminding Johnny Mercer that he'd been promising for years to write a lyric for his composition 'Slow Mood'. Apparently Mercer replied that he'd written some words for the tune ages ago and that he'd go to his office and get them.

He came back 2 hours later and Eddie tackled him suggesting that he'd just written them and Johnny Mercer admitted that he'd done just that.

The vocal version was re-named 'Love's got me in a Lazy Mood' and they both had a hit with it in 1944.

Digby Fairweather

I saw the Gene Krupa Band several times at the Capitol Theatre in New York when Gene fronted the band and Roy Eldridge played drums. He was a very useful drummer.

Buddy Rich

In my opinion Lester Young was the most exciting person ever in jazz, although I would agree that Louis Armstrong's contribution was earlier and greater.

The story I like about Lester Young is when he was working some place in the Mid West as a guest with a local band. Right from the start of the evening the trumpet player was saying things like, 'Prez, this reminds me of the old days.' He kept on like this throughout the evening, although he was playing badly as he was drinking too much.

Lester Young had never even seen this trumpet player before and was slowly becoming angry. Eventually, the trumpet player asked Prez when the last time was that they had played together, and Prez said, 'Tonight!'

Barney Kessel

Lester Young was a very sensitive man as we all know. Well, he had a problem when he wanted to leave Count Basie's band. He didn't want to offend Bill Basie by giving him the normal fourteen days' notice, so one night he stuck his head around

Basie's dressing room door and said, 'Basie, in one month's time, I'll have been out of this band two weeks.'

Humphrey Lyttelton

The New Orleans clarinettist Pete Fountain did so well that he bought a Rolls Royce. The trouble was, so many people ribbed him about it that he went out and bought a complete chauffeur's uniform so that he could drive around in peace.

Yank Lawson

One of the highlights of my life was the six years I worked with Oscar Peterson and Ray Brown.

Soon after I had joined them they noticed that I usually close my eyes when I take a solo. One night we were playing some tune where I had a long solo break before going into my choruses. All of a sudden I realised I was playing alone, and when I opened my eyes there were Oscar and Ray sitting in the front row.

Herb Ellis

Monty Alexander told me of the time he found himself alone in an elevator with Thelonious Monk, who was in front of the controls. Monty couldn't understand why the lift kept going up and down in an erratic way until he realised that Monk was using the controls as a calculator.

Humphrey Lyttelton

The only time I met Bobby Hackett was on an American radio programme something like this. They played him a trumpet record and he didn't recognise himself. Now that should give encouragement to anyone who appears on *Jazz Score*.

Benny Green

The Bobby Hackett story I like is the one about the night a gang of musicians at Condon's were trying to get the ever-polite Hackett to say something bad about somebody, in fact anybody. After exhausting all the well-known monsters and conmen connected with the American jazz scene, in desperation somebody asked him what he thought of Adolf Hitler. After a considerate pause, Hackett replied, 'Well, he was tops in his field.'

Digby Fairweather

There was a famous recording session made at Capitol Studios by some of their artistes. The record came out under the name of Ten Cats and a Mouse.

I know Peggy Lee played drums and Benny Carter and Eddie Miller switched instruments so Benny played tenor and Eddie played alto. I think Billy May played trombone.

Humphrey Lyttelton

Harry Levine's Barefoot Dixieland Philharmonic: the only thing I know about that band is that Dinah Shore did her first broadcast with them.

Barney Kessel

Sure, I worked the Onyx Club. That was on 52nd Street in the days when you could listen to music all night long because all the clubs were next door to each other. Everybody was swinging. Now they're ice skating: the Rockefeller Center is built over that site.

Slim Gaillard

In jazz, it has been quite usual for musicians under contract to one record company to record for another anonymously.

Early in his career, Louis Armstrong was caught out. His recording boss recognised his playing and confronted him. Louis said, 'That's not me . . . but I won't do it again.'

Humphrey Lyttelton

Trumpeter 'Bozo' Bose was one of those legendary trumpet players, and most of the legends involved alcohol. For example, when he was a Decca house musician in the 1930s he played in a quintet fondly known as the Falling-down Five. However, the story I like is how he was dragged from the sea almost half-drowned when he was carrying out an experience of trying to play his trumpet to the fish.

Digby Fairweather

▶ Eddie South was undoubtably the most technically able of all the jazz violinists. He toured England in 1930 with his 'Alabamians'.

There's a lovely story about the Guy Lombard Orchestra. Apparently they used to play for dancing at society jobs, where they used unbelievably long arrangements which were selections of tunes segued together and lasting anything up to two hours.

One night one of the guys pleaded that he must get off the stand to visit a toilet. 'Shut up,' said Lombardo, 'you knew about this job six weeks ago.'

Ronnie Scott

Many years ago, when I was living in Hollywood, I used to sit in at Billy Bird's, which billed itself as 'the Jazz Corner of the

World'. Sometimes I would just sit and listen to Art Tatum playing piano. On several of these occasions I was joined by a young teenager. That young man is now called André Previn.

Slim Gaillard

There's a story, probably apocryphal, about Duke Ellington at the Cotton Club in Harlem, which was run by gangsters. At one point clarinettist Barney Bigard left Duke to join Jelly Roll Morton, whose band was playing across the road. On his first night with Morton he was playing away when the doors burst open and two 'heavies' in wide-brimmed hats marched in, picked him up, still playing, carried him across the road and dumped him back in Duke's band, where he stayed for the next twelve years.

Humphrey Lyttelton

I worked with Lou McGarity in the World's Greatest Jazz Band. He was a fine trombone player who could also play 'Country' fiddle. He didn't class himself as a violin player.

Bob Wilber

Eddie South most likely had the best technique of all the jazz violinists. He had absolutely perfect pitch. Also he started singing in unison with his fiddle some time before Slam Stewart started doing the same thing with his bass.

Slim Gaillard

There's a story that high-note trumpet specialist Cat Anderson and trombonist Lawrence Brown from the Ellington Band had a disagreement one night in the middle of a concert. Actually, they were behind the band rolling on the floor when Duke left the piano, walked round the back of the band saying, 'Boys, boys. If I'd known you were doing the cabaret, I'd have written something special for you.'

Alan Elsdon

Hot Lips Page was a great dropper of bricks. There's a story of how one night Cole Porter walked into the club where he was leading the band. Lips gave this big spiel over the microphone about how honoured they were etc. – 'And as a tribute we'd like to play one of Mr Porter's wonderful compositions.' He picked up his trumpet and went straight into Gershwin's 'Embraceable You'.

Benny Green

In an interview with Steve Voce, Jack Sheldon reminisced about the good times he had playing in Stan Kenton's Orchestra, one of five trumpets. 'On fifth trumpet,' he said, 'you didn't have to worry too much about playing the written music. The band was so loud you could just sit there and play anything.'

Humphrey Lyttelton

It is most likely true that Johnny Hodges stopped playing soprano saxophone with the Ellington Band back in 1940 because Duke refused to pay him 'doubling' money. However, I can assure you that he played soprano sax at least once after that, albeit ten years later. The Ellington Band was playing a theatre in Boston, and some of them, including Hodges, came down to the club I was playing after their show. Rab (Rabbit) borrowed my soprano and played like a dream.

Incidentally, I have heard an alternative story of how Johnny Hodges acquired the nickname Rabbit. The conventional theory is that it came about because he enjoyed salad sandwiches, but I heard it was because, as a youngster, he could outrun the truancy officers during his school-days.

Bob Wilber

In the old days George Wein ran the Storyville Club in Boston, where he used to book all the great jazz soloists – with himself, naturally, on piano. But Lester Young made him audition first.

Another time Ruby Braff was playing in the club and he turned around at one point and said, George. Just play the notes, don't try to express yourself.'

Humphrey Lyttelton

▶ 'Now Mr Hodges, can you see that?' Duke Ellington helping 'Rabbit'.

There's a story about Wingy Manone when he was still in New Orleans. He was contracted to provide a 9-piece band in a very low budget joint where they got the minimum rates per man.

He booked a guitar player called Snoozer Quinn who had only one eye, but he was a good player. He also booked the famous New Orleans bass player Joe Loyocano who had a false leg, and of course, Wingy had only one arm. Indeed, the rest of the band were pretty decrepit with odd bits missing – an ear lobe here and a finger there.

At the end of the week, when Wingy got paid, the money only covered eight men. When he complained the manager said, 'I reckon you're just about one whole man short.'

Humphrey Lyttelton

That was Illinois Jacquet on tenor saxophone. Amongst the American jazz fraternity he is known as The Beast.

Herb Ellis

Clarinettist Irving Fazola took his stage-name from the notes FA-SO-LA in the tonic sol-fa scale. His real name was Irving Prestopnik.

Humphrey Lyttelton

We worked with Joe Venuti at the Newport Jazz Festival in 1968 – a wonderful experience.

The Venuti story I like is the one about how he found himself on the same bill as Paul Whiteman soon after having left the Whiteman orchestral circus. Apparently at that time Whiteman had a routine whereby he opened his show on a totally blacked-out stage while he conducted with a weeny light at the end of his baton. Gradually the lights would come up to reveal this army of musicians in amongst the harps and timpani.

Well, Joe Venuti remembered this opening routine and, being the famous practical joker he was, he insisted on the same lighting effect when his little quintet went on during the interval. The only difference was that a huge lamp was to be seen swinging around the stage, and as the lights came up all was revealed. Joe Venuti was conducting four men with a fishing rod.

Alex Welsh

Red Nichols wasn't too popular with the jazz musicians in the late 1920s when he seemed hell bent on becoming a 'society' bandleader.

At one point he ordered his musicians to fit themselves out with starchy beige suits and pricey suede shoes . . . at their own expense. Eddie Condon and George Wettling were in that band, and on the first night in their new uniforms Eddie played guitar with his right foot up on a chair and the other hidden behind a music stand. Behind the drums, only George's left foot was visible. They were sharing one pair of band shoes.

Humphrey Lyttelton

BRITISH MUSICIANS

ABROAD

J azz music is now global and the | class. This chapter deals with some of
best British musicians are world | their experiences whilst touring abroad.

When I was working the Atlantic liners in 1947, Harry Klein
and I went to the Three Deuces in New York to see Charlie
Parker. We were both completely knocked out by the wonderful music. Harry, despite being the most unassuming of
men, plucked up enough courage to congratulate Parker on
his saxophone playing, to which he replied, 'Lend me fifty
dollars.'

Ronnie Scott

I first met Gerry Mulligan in New York when I was the bass
player in a piano-less quartet he was rehearsing. Dropping the
piano was a pretty unique concept for that kind of music in
those days. The idea didn't catch on in New York, so Gerry
went out to the West Coast and the rest is history.

Peter Ind

When I was touring the States with my band in 1959, we were
travelling overnight after a concert when we came across a
roadhouse miles from anywhere which had banner lights across

the building announcing the appearance of the Stan Kenton Orchestra. Naturally, we stopped for a break and went inside.

The twenty-one-piece Kenton Band was squeezed onto a stand in a room no bigger than the back room at the Bull's Head, Barnes. On each table was a notice saying, 'Patrons are requested to moderate their conversation so as not to distract the artistes.'

Humphrey Lyttelton

In 1953 I spent many months playing residencies in Paris at the same time as Lil Hardin was living there. She was originally a tailoress, in fact she used to make Louis Armstrong's suits during the time she was married to him.

We had a great time going around together buying material which we would make up on her sewing machine. Afterwards, she would cook us pork chops and rice in the hotel.

Beryl Bryden

I lived in Australia for much of the 1960s and during that time I got to know the Graeme Bell Band very well.

I loved the book by Johnny Sangster, one of their earlier drummers who came to Britain with the band in the early 1950s. In it he tells of how they were in Japan in 1954 playing for the troops on recreational leave from the Korean War and how a certain Aussie major taught the band a few useful phrases in Japanese so they could break the ice when they visited any of the local bars. One phrase which appealed to Johnny was – 'My word, you're pretty and what an elegant establishment you have here'. So that evening he went out for a drink with some of the band and he tried out his Japanese. He couldn't believe it when he was immediately ejected from the bar without his feet touching the ground by a couple of Sumo-like bouncers.

Later he found out that what he'd been taught to say was – 'Undress now, my friend will pay'.

Campbell Burnap

In 1980 I did a tour of Holland with a band backing Beryl Bryden. One weekend we were playing on an open-air bandstand at the seaside resort of Scheveningen. Anyway, before Beryl sang 'West End Blues' she announced that we should all maintain thirty seconds silence as a tribute to Louis Armstrong.

Fine, so we're standing there being respectful when all of a sudden the silence is broken by an outburst of hysterical laughter from the drummer, Tony Allen, who was pointing to the sky with tears running down his cheeks. Above us was a small aeroplane towing one of those aerial advertisements, which read 'DUREX – THE BEST THERE IS'.

Digby Fairweather

I met a band in Germany who called themselves The Drakes of Dixieland. When I queried how they came by their name they told me there was a band in America which they much admired called The Ducks of Dixieland. Of course, they meant The Dukes of Dixieland.

Monty Sunshine

On my very first visit to New York in the late 1940s, I went to see the Bill Harris – Charlie Ventura Sextet at the Three Deuces in 52nd Street. I'll never forget the doorman, who was called Pincus. He had a long overcoat, peaked cap and smoked a cigar. The funny thing is that no matter what time of the night or day you passed him, he had the same spiel: 'Come on in, folks, you're just in time for the complete show.'

The last time I saw him was in 1978 outside another club. He had the same coat, the same cap and probably the same cigar butt. I wasn't at all surprised to be assured that I was 'just in time for the complete show'.

Ronnie Scott

Thelonious Monk was everyone's idea of the taciturn modern jazz musician – dark glasses, goatee beard and all. We toured in America in 1959 on a coach that had my band, Lennie Tristano's Quintet and the Monk Quartet on board. Lee Konitz was with Tristano, and at the Nice Jazz Festival a year or two ago he reminded me of an incident en route.

Monk sat on the coach day after day totally silent, with his wife Nellie equally silent beside him. Then one day, a dog or something ran across the road, the driver hit the brakes and all the baggage fell off the racks. Monk stood up, said, 'Well, shut my mouth wide open,' sat down and never spoke another word for the rest of the tour.

Humphrey Lyttelton

While I was living in Australia the Eddie Condon Band came to Sydney and, naturally, all the local jazz musicians were very excited. In fact, many of us were waiting outside the theatre for their arrival. Pee Wee Russell actually fell out of a taxi holding his clarinet and played most of the evening with one hand while the other gripped the piano for support.

The Australian drummer Len Barnard summed him up by saying that Pee Wee's face looked like the last four bars of 'Tiger Rag'.

Campbell Burnap

I was in the back of a taxi with Victor Feldman in Hollywood on the way to see the Curtis Counce Quintet when the driver turned around and said, 'Hey, are you guys British? Do you know a guitarist called Dave Goldberg?' So we assured him that not only did we know Dave Goldberg, but that he was also a very good friend of ours. It turned out that Dave had shared an apartment with this taxi driver some years earlier when he had lived in the States.

As if that was not unusual enough, when we did get to the club and I went to the bar I realised that the barman used to be one of the Dead End Kids.

Ronnie Scott

While I was on tour with my band in Germany, my trumpet player, Mike Cotton, spotted our roadie-cum-driver taking

► A face like the last 4 bars of 'Tiger Rag' is the way one Australian jazz musician described Charles Ellsworth 'Pee Wee' Russell whose unique clarinet style became ever more asthmatic over the years.

some pills to keep himself awake. So Mike warned him that those sort of pills could become addictive. 'Don't be silly', said our driver, 'my father has been taking these pills for over twenty-five years.'

Acker Bilk

At one time I lived in Spain, where I owned a bar. One day I received a letter from William Charles Disley, the guitarist, saying that he intended visiting me and was there anything I would like brought out. I wrote back immediately asking for a Double Gloucester cheese and a piano.

About two weeks later I was sitting in the bar 'entertaining' the local sergeant of police, who was beginning to call on me too frequently, when the door opened and a large Double Gloucester cheese entered with Disley underneath it. Disley then informed me that the piano was in the car with an actor asleep on top of it.

The Spanish police sergeant was most intrigued by all this and in particular with the car, which was a 1935 Rolls Royce shooting break. Disley offered him a ride in this splendid vehicle. Well, actually, he made a gesture which he interpreted as an offer for a ride. They drove around the town with the sergeant waving to all his friends and much consequent kudos gained.

Anyway, I never saw the sergeant again; he must have thought I was a 'good egg' and left me alone. So I gained a Double Gloucester cheese and a piano and lost an unwanted policeman all in one fell swoop, thanks to Diz Disley.

Dick Charlesworth

When I was with the Kenny Clarke–Francy Boland Big Band I remember missing a flight to Budapest in Hungary. Actually, the gig was about 200 miles from Budapest. Anyway, I caught the next flight possible and they laid on the number 1 Hungarian rally driver to get me there. We did 200 miles in about one and a half hours and I went on stage gibbering with fear.

Ronnie Scott

There's a story from way back in the 1950s, when Dill Jones was playing piano with Tommy Whittle's Band in Paris. At that time there were scores of unknown American musicians in Paris, many of them hip-looking guys in dark glasses and berets but without much talent to match. Dill used to get enraged at the way they were lionised by the local musicians, often for no other reason than that they were American.

There was a bass-player called Lloyd Thompson who had made a record with Charlie Parker. One night he turned up at the club where Tommy and Dill were working; everyone made a big fuss, and eventually he was invited to sit in. I won't attempt the Welsh accent, but as Lloyd Thompson got up on the bandstand Dill rose majestically from the piano and said, 'I don't care if you have played with bloody Charlie Parker . . . you'd better bloody well swing when you play with me, boy!'

Humphrey Lyttelton

Some of the TV adverts in America are outrageous. I once saw a cigarette advert which featured this very pretty girl saying 'I've tried everything, but I prefer a Camel.'

Ronnie Scott

About five years ago I was at the Nice Festival playing with Humph's band and after the blow I went off with my wife Pat for a drink in town. On the way we passed an old guy playing violin in the street. We listened for a few minutes, put a handful of francs in his hat and moved on to this bar where all the British musicians generally go.

Soon after, Digby [Fairweather] and some others came in and we started a jam session. The people really enjoyed it and some started dancing. After a while I noticed the violin player dancing. As he passed us he threw a few francs on the table.

John Barnes

I remember touring Ireland with the Ted Heath Band when a chap came by and asked if we played requests. Ted told him he would try and asked him what he would like to hear. 'Oh, anything at all', said the Irishman.

Ronnie Scott

When I was in New Orleans in 1965 I had a three-dollar music lesson from the veteran trumpet player Punch Miller; you know he got his name because he had a sister Judy. The music lesson turned out to be an hour in Miller's kitchen talking about the old days. I suggested that he must have had a lot of fun in the early days in Chicago with his contemporaries like J. C. Higginbotham and Henry 'Red' Allen. 'No,' he said, 'they would spend all day in their hotel rooms practising.'

Campbell Burnap

The first time I played at Massey Hall was with the local orchestra, the Toronto Symphony. I got there early because I'd heard that you could get bad echoes and I was worried about the sound system. I wandered around for a while, but I couldn't find anyone to ask about the sound system except for an old lady with grey hair and a floral hat who was stumbling around about five string desks back. The musicians were just starting to arrive in the building and I thought that perhaps she was the mother of one of the second violinists.

Having no one else to ask, I called out to her, enquiring if she could help me. 'Scuse me, dearie', she replied in a broad cockney accent, which rather shook me to start off with. 'Hang on', she said, 'I'd better come down nearer, I'm a bit deaf.'

Well, after a bit of shouting to each other, she turned out to be in charge of the sound system, which worked surprisingly well.

John Dankworth

Many years ago I worked in a club in Palma, Majorca. The drummer in the band was married to the daughter of Robert Graves, the author. In fact, Robert Graves lived in a small village in the centre of the island. I'll never forget the first time I met him, which was when I was invited to the Graves' home for lunch. The first thing Robert said to me was 'What's the pot situation in London these days?'

Ronnie Scott

I did a summer cruise around the Greek islands which finished up in Egypt. I'll never forget the trombonist Terry Pitts fancied having his photograph taken sitting on a camel. He got into a great haggle about money with the camel handler because he only wanted to sit on it and not go for a ride. Anyway, they agreed on one dollar, so Tony clambers on and at the command the camel stands up.

Good, photograph taken, but the camel handler wanted five dollars to make the camel sit down again.

Alan Elsdon

Of course Marian McPartland left these shores ages ago when she married Jimmy. Did you know she comes from my home-town of Windsor? She is a from a musical family – the Dysons. Her great uncle, Sir Frederick Dyson, was Mayor of Windsor and a distinguished cellist. They used to play in all the amateur musical shows and her father was the conductor.

Humphrey Lyttelton

Naturally, I had a guide dog when I was working in the States.

One day I was flying from New York to Chicago with the dog when the captain of the plane recognised me, as he had seen me playing a few nights before. He came over for a chat and finished up by taking the dog, with its special control lead, for a walk around the outside of the aircraft so that it could have a pee before take-off. I heard that when he was spotted through the windows several people got off and waited for the next flight.

Eddie Thompson

I remember travelling as a guest with the Ronnie Scott Sextet when they visited America in exchange for the Eddie Condon Band in 1957.

We sailed on the *Queen Elizabeth* but, as there was a dock strike in New York, we were diverted to Halifax in Nova Scotia. From there we were flown to New York, but as there were so many passengers to squeeze into these planes everybody was restricted to one suitcase only. Obviously we had to take the instruments, so we had to wear every item of clothing we had taken with us. We all looked like Jimmy Rushing.

Benny Green

Some years ago I met Art Blakey in Times Square and he suggested that I come down to the Five Spot that night where

Outside the Salle Pleyel, Paris 1949. *L to R:* Norman Burns, Johnny Dankworth, Joe Muddel, Laurie Morgan and Ronnie Scott.

he was working. So I went as arranged, and while my eyes were getting accustomed to the gloom a voice called out, 'Hi, Ronnie', and without looking I yelled back, 'Art Blakey!'

I turned around to see it was Elvin Jones.

Ronnie Scott

At one time the Ken Colyer Band was both incredibly popular and influential in Germany. The clarinet player was Ian Wheeler, who used to bob up and down and pump his elbows in and out, and the trombonist was Mac Duncan, who used to sway from side to side. Even to this day, when you tour Germany, you can see clarinet players bobbing up and down and swaying trombonists.

Alan Elsdon

One night we were playing out in the Middle East, I think it was Abu Dhabi, anyway Georgie Fame was staying at our hotel and he was talked into sitting in with us for a jam session.

We were playing outside by the swimming pool and certain people complained because of the noise at 1.00 am. There were more than enough guests enjoying the music and they carried all the gear in and set us up in the hotel foyer. After a while some irate guests came storming down the stairs threatening to call the manager. The manager turned out to be a total jazz nut and he sat in on drums for the next hour.

Acker Bilk

Back in the 1950s my band played a short tour of Norway. When we were in Oslo, a bus collected us from our hotel and we were driven about eight miles outside of the city to a lovely pine building in a forest. Unfortunately, the concert was a disaster as hardly anybody turned up.

Afterwards, I asked the promoters why we hadn't played somewhere in the centre of Oslo. The few fans who managed to find us out in the forest said that the big jazz concerts were usually held in the central City Hall. Well, it appears that this hall has a huge semi-circular stage fringed by niches containing the busts of Norway's national heroes. Apparently, the last British band to appear there was that of drummer Joe Daniels. He did what he called his 'drumnastics', in which he drummed on everything in sight – the floor, the walls, the furniture, everything. That night he drummed all over the Norwegian national heroes, knocking a few of their noses off in the process. So we played in this forest . . .

Humphrey Lyttelton

The first trip I made abroad with the Ted Heath Orchestra was to Sweden. When we landed in Stockholm, the local musicians had laid on a reception for what was supposed to be the greatest big band in Europe at that time.

I remember when we heard Stan Hasselgård play clarinet, the Heath Band visibly paled and Ted didn't call out any clarinet features on the whole tour.

Ronnie Scott

A couple of years back I went over to New York for the Brass

Convention, and then I went on to LA to stay with Manny Klein. While I was there he gave me an album produced by Toots Camarata called 'Tutti's Trumpets', and Manny was one of the featured trumpet players.

I was able to tell him how Toots Camarata had really given the Ted Heath Orchestra a leg-up back in 1946 when, as MD for the film musical *London Town*, he had featured us along with Sid Field and a twelve-year-old Petula Clark.

Ronnie and I made a lot of money out of that film. I saw it on television last week – it was bloody awful.

Kenny Baker

Collin Bates, the pianist who worked with George Melly for so many years, recently returned to Australia after an absence of twenty years. He has written a letter back describing how many things have improved there, particularly in the theatre and music world.

However, he did say that the drinking scene was still pretty primitive. He said he saw a notice in a bar which stated 'Drink "Downunder Brandy", the Australian brandy without that nasty cognac taste'.

Alan Elsdon

When I was in America with the Chris Barber Band I walked into our drummer's hotel room and was confronted by Graham [Burbidge] totally naked, apart from a belt and holster, pointing a gun at me. When I asked him what the hell he was doing, he told me about Sammy Davis Junior standing in front of a TV set and every time a scene changed he would draw his gun as fast as possible. So I asked him about being nude and he told me his clothes slowed down his action.

Monty Sunshine

I was being taken around New York on a sightseeing trip by Zoot Sims and Al Cohn. Al had his camera with him and he wanted to take some pictures of me and Zoot together. Well, you know Al Cohn has a glass eye, so Zoot turned to him and

▶ 'Acker in Par-is, chestnuts in bloss-om,
Scrumpy on tables, un-der the trees.'

said, 'Make sure you put your good eye to the viewfinder or
the photograph won't come out.'

Ronnie Scott

Lennie Hastings used to break an audience up every time he
left the drum kit to come out in front of the Alex Welsh Band
to sing one of his Richard Tauber songs in his own special
German. I can see him now with a monocle in his eye and his
trousers rolled up to the knee. Actually, at parties he would

dress up in a storm-trooper's uniform to sing these songs.

One time they were having a party in an hotel in Germany when there were complaints about the noise, and eventually the hotel manager phoned through to say that he had called the police. Almost immediately there was a knock on the door and two big Bavarian policemen presented themselves, saying, 'Vee haf heard there is much noise 'ere.' To which Lennie responded, 'Nix fishstain' [nicht verstehen/no understand].

'Stupid. Vee are speaking Englisch to you,' said a policeman.

Acker Bilk

There used to be a Scots comic actor called Monty Landis who was a great jazz fan.

Years ago I ran into him in New York and he drove me around for a couple of days in a superb Cadillac convertible. I remember one night we went to Harlem to see the Frank Foster Band with Johnny Coles on trumpet. Apparently, Monty had rented this car in Los Angeles about eight months earlier and the police in a dozen states were looking for him.

Actually, I saw him in an episode of *The Monkees* since that time, so perhaps they never found him.

Ronnie Scott

Jazz bands get some bizarre jobs as we all know, but one of the most unusual I have heard of recently concerned the Piccadilly Six, the British band domiciled in Switzerland.

They were hired for the ceremonial opening of an extension to the sewage works in Zürich. So they set themselves up on this temporary stage conveniently situated some distance away from where all the VIPs were obviously going to be entertained. Then comes the opening ceremony and a sheet is pulled back which has been covering a mock-up water closet with a chain. Some local dignitary stands up and says a few suitable words, the band starts to play and the dignitary pulls the chain.

At this point the flood gates open and the band is surrounded, indeed marooned, by a mass of, how can I describe it – sewage?

Dick Charlesworth

There is a marvellous band from Cuba called Irakere, affectionately known as Earache. We've had them at the club several times. The leader is called Chucho Valdés; his real name is Jesus but Chucho sounds better.

I first saw them in Havana in 1984 when I was in Cuba playing a festival. They're lovely people the Cubans, but I stayed in an hotel where I used to phone room service about 8 am to ask for coffee but it never arrived before 11 am. I got fed up with this after about three days, so I arranged with the night porter that I give him a note asking for coffee at 8 am and that he could give it to the breakfast guy when he came on duty.

About 6 am the next day I got a telephone call which said, 'Señor Scott, don't forget to phone room service.'

Ronnie Scott

I've met some very fine musicians in Belgium, which is strange for such an odd country.

Ronnie Scott

When Geoff Sowden was with my band in the early 1960s he bought the most dreadful watch while we were on tour in Germany. It really was a load of rubbish, which didn't cost him much more than the equivalent of a pound. Anyway, he wouldn't leave this watch alone. All day long he was checking the time, and I swear he wound it up five or six times a day.

Soon after we returned we played a concert at the Liverpool Empire in front of a capacity crowd. It came to the point where we played 'Basin Street Blues' and the arrangement required Geoff to play a bravura intro on trombone and then Beryl Bryden would come in with the vocal. Well, half-way through the introduction Geoff's watch actually exploded and bits flew all over the stage. Now, anybody normal would carry on playing. Not Geoff. Almost in tears, he was on his hands and knees picking up bits of his watch, and 'Basin Street Blues' ground to a chaotic halt.

Monty Sunshine